Deep & Simple

Deep
&
Simple

A Spiritual Path
for Modern Times

by Bo Lozoff

compiled and edited by Joshua Lozoff

foreword by Jarvis Jay Masters

Human Kindness Foundation

ISBN: 978-0-9614444-6-4
Library of Congress Catalog Card Number: 99-90204

Printed in the U.S.A.

Editor: Joshua Lozoff
Cover design: Nancy Kaiser, the Plough Publishing House
Photos: Bob Shrager

fourth printing 2009
80,000 copies in print

Copies of this book are sent free to prisoners and other indigents throughout the world. The Human Kindness Foundation is a non-profit organization which sponsors the Prison-Ashram Project and other programs promoting basic kindness and spiritual sanity. 100% of the proceeds from book sales and donations go to support these programs.

Human Kindness Foundation
PO Box 61619
Durham, NC 27715
Online at www.humankindness.org

Other Books By Bo Lozoff:

We're All Doing Time (Human Kindness Foundation, ©1985)
(published in Spanish as *Todos Estamos Encarcelados,* ©1989)
(published in French as *Nous Sommes Tous Dans Une Prison,* © 1995)
(published in Italian as *Siamo Tutti in Priogione,* © 1998)
(published in Dutch as *We Zitten Allemaal Vast,* © 2006)

Lineage and Other Stories (Human Kindness Foundation, ©1988)

Just Another Spiritual Book (Human Kindness Foundation, ©1990)

THE FOLLOWING ITEMS ARE <u>NOT</u> AVAILABLE FREE:

It's a Meaningful Life, It Just Takes Practice (Viking/Penguin, ©2000)

The Wonderful Life of a Fly Who Couldn't Fly (Hampton Roads, ©2002) – Bo's first children's book, beautifully illustrated.

To my family at Kindness House,
who have come from all walks of life
to commit themselves to
the deep and simple way.

And to Josh & Melissa, and
Arjun & Janaki, for
having the courage to say
" 'Til Death Do Us Part"
and mean it.

Acknowledgments

My son, Josh, worked on this book for over a year with great affection for the reader. He pored over my writings spanning ten years, listened to many hours of taped talks, and reached into his heart to develop a clear and direct stream of thought which I could never have pulled together without his help.

My wife, Sita, and the other members of my community took on a lot of extra work so that Josh and I could finish *Deep & Simple*. They have also allowed their lives to be the laboratory in which these principles and practices are tested in the fire of the real world.

I have recently been inspired by the Bruderhof Communities, whose truly spiritual Christianity is both a blessing and challenge to the modern world. Charles Moore, of the Bruderhof's Plough Publishing, arranged for one of his community's talented graphic artists, Nancy Kaiser, to design this book cover as a generous expression of support for our work. We are very grateful to them both.

I thank the volunteers who transcribed tapes into writings, including Justin Lozoff, Pam Miller, and Achsah Reeder. And to the countless spiritual seekers and pilgrims who have written letters, attended talks, shared their problems and solutions and faith with me, and of course to my mother, father, and Guru, I say thanks and a hearty *Jaya* — spiritual victory to us all.

Table of Contents

12 Practices for a Deep & Simple Life

Foreword

by Jarvis Jay Masters

In 1991, when I first read *We're All Doing Time*, I had no idea that Bo's words would be a constant companion to me all these years since. But they have been. His writings then, as now, in *Deep & Simple*, are about all of us. In a deep, simple, clear voice, Bo reminds us that no matter where we are as human beings, whether in suburbia or on death row, there is a goodness inherent in the human spirit.

It's easy to follow, in this great book, the steps to a deep spiritual awakening which simply refuses to shield us from the fact that we are all somehow connected. We all matter, we all count, and we are all able to make a difference. There are paths in life, and our reason for existence can be found within each of us.

There are chapters in *Deep & Simple* which made me feel as though I could sit and hear Bo's voice as if he was the best cellie I've ever had (not that I wish my ol' friend could share a San Quentin death cell with me). But these teachings and practices are like a beautiful collage of insights that filled my thoughts and reaffirmed my faith that life is simply what we are able to make of it; and that even I, someone on death row, can still be of enormous benefit. All our human imperfections can truly be put to great use, and we can even give hope to the hopeless.

Although the ideas in this book may seem simple to realize while our eyes are focused on these pages, it is just like Bo to make sure we remember, "Anyone looking for an easy, painless way through life should burn this book immediately."

To this I say, "Right on, Bo!" Too often we may read quick-fix books and feel so excited, ready to try this or that, and then wait, sitting on our posteriors hoping to get out of uncomfortable situations or whatever rat-holes we find ourselves in, whether it be our mental or physical imprisonment. It's as if we watch a blank screen and expect results. This is not what *Deep & Simple* is about. Bo never lets us forget that there are mountains to climb, tough, rugged mountains that include every possible human situation, imaginable or unimaginable. We can begin the climb by becoming connected to a spiritual path that will lead to our being awakened and fully alive.

While I was reading *Deep & Simple* one morning, I kept glancing out my cell window, where I can see a large hillside just beyond the prison gates. An inmate work crew was out there, climbing it slowly, hoeing weeds and brush. When they were halfway up the hill, I became absorbed in Bo's account of taking his son Josh and a group of other kids from Josh's school to the mountains of North Carolina for a wilderness training course. They spent five days there doing ropes courses, rock climbing and other physical challenges.

To see the spiritual journey in this, while watching the steady, tireless work of the men outside my cell window, I got a strong feeling of what Bo meant by developing inner qualities. If I or anyone could be challenged to clear out a whole hillside by chopping down weeds and brush, and for only seventeen cents an hour, then no less is required to meet any of life's spiritual climb — a climb that is filled with all kinds of possibilities for doing something meaningful, lasting and inwardly fulfilling with our lives. The hard work those men were doing would probably never have been done on their own. Who would, without a reason? Yet a book such as this one empowers us with reasons to do many hard things.

More importantly, *Deep & Simple* makes a profound connection between what a genuine spiritual life is able to teach us today, and what every great religion and tradition has sought to share with each of us along this path. We all have names for these teachings, whether we call them holy scriptures, spiritual truths, universal laws, or whatever. They all come down to *faith*, the most sacred of all human trusts and beliefs. Bo shines a great light of understanding on the nature of true faith — that it is something higher and more powerful than ourselves; that faith holds no attachment to particular outcomes or results; that faith is not about miracles which we may wish would come shining down into our lives. Faith is the fullness to realize that each moment of our lives is a gift; that the whole of our lives is a spiritual journey, whether in our darkest hours or brightest joys.

I think the reader will see that *Deep & Simple* is truly "a spiritual path for modern times." Bo is not afraid to share some of the turbulent experiences that occurred in his early life — which so many of us will be able to identify with, like seeing ourselves in a mirror. He writes about the Human Kindness Foundation and his own three-fold path: simple living, service to humanity, and a deep belief in daily spiritual practice. And he provides many good examples of how we can start where we are, right now, instead of fooling ourselves into needing to find a perfect launch pad. I, for one, know there aren't any.

I truly hope that *Deep & Simple* will be read by everyone, especially by those locked up and down in the prison system. Let ol' Bo cell up with you for however long it takes you to see that there is a difference we can all make, not only for ourselves, but for others as well. Perhaps in some things, there are no stronger voices or examples than ours. I thank Bo for reminding us of this.

San Quentin, Ca
January 1999

*T*hose who wish to know the truth take joy in doing the work and service that comes to them.

Having completed it, they take joy in cleansing and feeding themselves.

Having cared for others and themselves, they then turn to the master for instruction.

*T*his simple path leads to peace, virtue, and abundance.

— Lao Tzu, *Hua Hu Ching*

Introduction:

A Three-Fold Path

Deep and simple. That's the razor's edge. We can easily be deep but not simple, brooding over the mysteries of life or over our own problems, emitting a serious, heavy presence as though we carry the weight of the world on our shoulders. This is a path of struggle and confusion.

Or we can fall into being simple but not deep, like many "new-age" followers, who naively believe that by keeping their minds solely on positive thoughts, they will attune themselves to never-ceasing abundance, never-ending health and life, good times and happiness. Despite all its slogans and cheerleading, this is a path of fear and denial.

Being deep *and* simple is a very graceful balance which requires no less than all of our commitment, attention, and persistence. This is the path of the sages. This is the balance you and I can study and practice every moment of our lives, no matter what circumstances or environments we must face.

Long ago, I noticed three practical tips for deep and simple living which every great tradition seemed to hold in common: spiritual practice, simplicity, and a dedication to service. By spiritual practice, I mean we are reminded that reading and thinking are not enough; the sages and saints have left behind many methods which gradually bring about a profound awakening. By simplicity, I mean that we are advised to live modestly and not get too caught up in luxury or possessions, not to waste our divine energy on too much worldliness. By a dedication to service, I mean that we are encouraged to devote ourselves to the common good rather than merely self-centered success.

This book is organized along those threefold lines, although of course they can never be fully separated: The first section, *A Wide, Round Curve*, focuses on the role of spiritual practice in our real, day-to-day lives. The second section, *How Little We Need*, provides a few up-close views of what it takes to get off the merry-go-round of "more, bigger, better, newer." The third section, *Whatever I Can*, takes a look at dedicating our personal life to the common good.

Additionally, I have included *12 Practices for a Deep & Simple Life* as a fourth section so that, if you choose, you can immediately begin to apply some of the principles and ideas of this book. I have found great value in all of these practices and I hope you do, too.

I love the world's religious scriptures, and I believe with all my heart that they share more similarities than differences. None of them would find fault with a lifestyle of practice, simplicity, and service. None would find fault with the term "deep and simple." According to the world's great scriptures, the meaning of life is deep and the rules of life are simple.

I hope you are able to use this book as a friendly interfaith resource which does not compete or conflict with your religious views, but rather enriches and enlivens your beliefs and helps you to apply them even more effectively in your everyday life.

The Holy Ones promise us that we can become radiantly alive, unafraid, shining beacons of goodness and faith. You and I may look within and find that very hard to believe. Yet we do believe, even if we stubbornly pretend that we don't. We hold the divine spark in our hearts, and we are aching to let it become a blazing fire which consumes all our foolishness and despair. This ongoing challenge is the human spiritual journey we all share.

A Wide, Round Curve

Changes in attitude never come easily.
The development of love and
compassion is a wide, round curve that
can be negotiated only slowly, not a
sharp corner that can be turned all at
once.

It comes with daily practice.

—His Holiness, the Dalai Lama of Tibet

Make it Real

The master said there is one thing in this world which must never be forgotten.

It is as if a king had sent you to a country to carry out one special, specific task. You go to the country and you perform a hundred other tasks, but if you have not performed the task you were sent for, it is as if you have performed nothing at all.

So man has come into the world for a particular task, and that is his purpose. If he doesn't perform it, he will have done nothing.

— Rumi

What is that task? That one task which, if we don't perform, we will have done nothing? There's nothing mysterious about what Rumi, the great thirteenth-century Islamic mystic and poet, meant. The "task" is to be living life as a spiritual journey; it's to remember that life is solely, totally, a sacred, holy process, and that at the center of each of us, **our real nature is far bigger than even life and death.** Big and wonderful beyond imagining.

7

The task isn't to *complete* the journey; it's not to become enlightened, liberated, self-realized, etc. That's certainly the ultimate goal, but it's not fully within our control; there's a lot of unseen purification and Grace involved far beyond our understanding.

No, Rumi's use of the word "task" suggests something more immediate, something each of us is capable of choosing right now — like choosing to have *faith* in the inherent goodness, order and intelligence of every moment. No one can force us to trust in the Great Goodness; it's got to be our own free choice, a choice made with soft, compassionate eyes wide open to the cruelty and unhappiness going on around us.

When it's honest and strong, such faith brings us a peacefulness that connects us to something very deep and very real. That peacefulness itself is proof that such faith is a better choice — even in the daily, practical world — than fear, cynicism, or bitterness.

In January 1994, when the big earthquake shook Los Angeles, our son Josh was living out there. It hit at 4:30am, and at 5:30am, Josh called to let us know he was all right — a few things had fallen off the shelves, he had some broken glass to clean up, some cracks in the walls that didn't look too serious. He was spared the kinds of personal injuries or catastrophic damage suffered by thousands of his neighbors. Within hours he was free to be a helper, rather than one of the many who needed so much help.

Josh said he also called to thank us, because within seconds of being rattled awake, while lying in bed with the whole world shaking violently around him, he found his mind calm, focused on God, silently repeating our family mantra, "Ram" (one of the names of God in Hinduism).

Josh said the earthquake was a humbling reminder of how fragile and brief our physical lives are. Dozens of people died in that quake, and he surely could have been among them. He was very grateful that, in what may have been his final moments of life, his mind turned naturally to his personal spiritual practice. Rumi's "one thing which must never be forgotten" had indeed *not* been forgotten even in the throes of an earthquake. Josh's source of deepest peace was intact without frantic effort on his part.

Eat the Meal

It's in our worst times that spiritual work makes the biggest difference, and that's why it's so important to practice during ordinary times. If Josh hadn't done mantra practice to center his mind countless times during meditation, or while lying in bed, walking down the street, eating, driving his car, then how would a calm or clear state of mind stand a chance against "Ohhh SHIT!!! NOT ME!! NOT YET!!" during the suddenness of a major earthquake? (See Practice #4 on page 148 for working with mantras.)

Like anything else, Sacred Living requires practice — simple, down-to-earth, daily, time-honored methods of remembering, remembering, remembering.

The purpose of daily spiritual practice is simply to strengthen our awareness; to make **real and natural** — down to our bones and cells and thought waves — our awareness that life is a continuously perfect process.

We may *want* to be more aware of the Divine, we may *want* to be more in touch with the Sacred, we may *believe* in it — but then somebody rips us off or runs over our dog or insults our mother, or our house burns down. Life keeps happening in one way or another to make it too hard for us to actually **see** that everything's still all right; to actually **feel** our deepest faith, in those darkest hours.

> Reading spiritual books is like reading the menu at a restaurant. Don't forget you must eat the meal.
>
> — Chogyam Trungpa Rinpoche

Modern life has become so badly lopsided toward the conceptual, toward "knowing about," that many of us have lost sight entirely of the power of *being* instead. We tend to confuse knowledge with *wisdom*. We think that reading the menu is the same as eating the meal.

Yet every Great Tradition issues many, many warnings against this very lopsidedness. Jesus himself says at one point, "Oh Father, I thank you for concealing these truths from the clever and learned, and revealing them to the simple."

Every tradition echoes the same sentiment — something that points us toward an important distinction between *learning* on the one hand, and *transforming ourselves* on the other. Spiritual life has always been clearly about transformation. And because of this, it is not only un*help*ful to continue learning, learning, learning without deeply assimilating what we have learned, but can actually become quite a hindrance when our minds become so full of comparative ideas and views that we get further and further from true peace.

We can read a hundred spiritual books and be deeply touched, moved to tears, inspired, encouraged — but then what? Where does it all go during an earthquake, or when our deepest fears attack us with a vengeance? Daily practice is what helps us to take our highest awareness even down into our deepest dream states. Practices are how we gradually learn to eat the meal.

Ordinary Practice

It also takes practice to stop pushing all the buttons we have developed and defended for so many years; practice to dismantle all the things we habitually feel threatened by or attracted to — countless petty addictions, likes and dislikes which limit the easygoingness and joy which we could feel throughout every day.

A belief or an attitude is a great first step, but we must follow it up with daily practice. We must *remind* ourselves of what we believe in, we must find ways to deepen and strengthen those beliefs; we must see how they hold up under pressure. We must make spiritual practice part of our ordinary life experiences throughout each day.

It's really not that hard... . It just takes practice.

Take it on Faith

The darkness of the future is the necessary space for the exercise of our faith.

— A Carthusian Monk (11th century)

Developing a spiritual practice begins by choosing to have faith in something — an idea, a teacher, a saint, a religion, a prayer. We put our faith in something noble and then we take it into our real lives, into our strengths and weaknesses and hopes and fears and disappointments, and *work* with it.

A spiritual truth, an object of our faith, which doesn't hold up in a prison cell or during an earthquake, isn't a big enough truth. The Big Truths are true throughout any possible condition life can present to us.

When we choose faith, it doesn't mean that bad things no longer happen to us; it just means that there is no longer any cause for fear or bitterness in our pain. Fear implies we're unprotected, and bitterness implies something shouldn't have happened the way it did. Both are false to the person of faith.

Fear says, "You'd better watch out! It's dark up ahead!" But in daily practice of faith, you can remind yourself, "Of course it's dark up ahead! Up ahead is not my business; this moment is, and it's light enough for me to see right now."

We're like a coal miner carrying his light on his cap. Wherever he arrives, it's light enough for him to see. He doesn't look ahead and say, "But it's dark up there!" He knows that by the time he gets there, it will be light. This light by which we see comes from inside of us. So it makes more sense to work on brightening our light and keeping the batteries strong, than to worry about what's in the dark up ahead. The light only exists "here," wherever we are — never "there." And it only exists "now," never "then." Faith accepts this, fear refuses to.

Rejoice in the Unknown

Re-read the quote at the beginning of this chapter. Think about it. **If the future were *not* unknown, not covered in darkness, then there would be no free will and no need for faith.** If the whole mine were lit, the coal miner would have no use for his own light.

Our individual spiritual journey — the wrestling, the struggles against fears, weaknesses, and shadows — would be meaningless, because we'd see exactly how it's all going to turn out. Life itself would be meaningless if there were no possibility that our free choice could make a difference in the kind of future we will experience.

The "darkness of the future" — the fact that no one knows, no one has a guarantee of anything at all — is not a reason for fear, it's a cause for rejoicing, because it means our lives are important, it means all possibilities remain open to us. It is indeed the very ground, the absolute necessity, of all spirituality.

13

At a conference in Switzerland some years ago, a woman asked all the panelists, "How do you see the world fifty years from now?" They all answered from their own areas of expertise, except for His Holiness the Dalai Lama of Tibet. He spoke last, and said, **"Madam, I don't even know what kind of tea I'll be having with dinner tonight. How could I possibly know what will happen fifty years from now?"** And then he laughed and laughed. There is great peace and happiness in the absence of all fear and in the acceptance of our proper sphere of concern — doing our very best, shining our very brightest, in this one little spot we find ourselves in. That's all we're designed to do.

Ego's Kinfolk

The great enemy of faith is our own ego. Ego says, "Yeah, faith is fine for Sundays, but meanwhile, you need *me* to really watch out for you in the 'real world.' My uncle, Fear, will protect you. My brother, Anger, will defend you. My sister, Desire, will bring you pleasure. God's pretty busy, you know; but I'm paying attention to you alone. Who loves ya, baby?"

It's a persuasive pitch, but our own experience is what eventually forces us to realize it's a hype. What ego doesn't mention is what we *feel* like living with fear, anger, desire, greed, ambition, and other forms of ego-protection. We feel cut off. We feel constantly "apart *from*" instead of "a part *of.*" We feel like abandoned orphans in a chaotic, violent universe. When ego is our protector, when ego is what we have our strongest faith in, we feel rotten and lonely, as most of us know all too well by now.

Then, when we begin to see through the lies and try to make some changes through some honest spiritual searching, Ego's kinfolk turn the pressure up a notch. Ego's cousin, Doubt, says, "Oh, are you really going to believe in all that religious mumbo-jumbo? That's just stuff people convince themselves of in order to feel better! Don't be an idiot!" And Fear is right next to him saying, "Yeah, you don't want to make a fool of yourself, do you? Aren't you afraid of losing your edge?"

I see many people, even some of the most religious among us, abandoning true faith and replacing it with a qualified faith which rationalizes their hopelessness. They seem to be losing hope in perfection, in complete spiritual transformation. **Many clergymen — themselves having lost hope — have become essentially therapists instead of a gateway for their parishioners to reach the transcendent, Sacred Reality.** It breaks my heart to see so many beautiful people redefining the Divine in order to settle for less.

But God hasn't changed. Allah has not become divided. Buddha's Third Noble Truth (that there is a perfect state of being) hasn't become untrue. Christ hasn't died. Many of us are simply afraid to continue hoping for and having faith in what they promised us — a direct, perfect, totally fulfilling meeting with God. Please don't lose hope. Choose to have faith that there is indeed One Great Reality which hasn't the slightest imperfection or disappointment or confusion.

The way to truly experience it for yourself is to develop your spiritual practices, and then include every moment and every event of your life in your spiritual journey. No time out.

A Story of Compassionate Cruelty

Be grateful when what seems unkind comes from a wise person.

Once, a holy man, riding his donkey, saw a poisonous snake crawling into a sleeping man's mouth! He hurried, but he couldn't prevent it. He hit the man several blows with his club.

The man woke terrified and ran beneath an apple tree with many rotten apples on the ground.

"Eat! You miserable wretch! Eat."

"Why are you doing this to me?"

"Eat more, you fool."

"I've never seen you before! Who are you? Do you have some inner quarrel with my soul?"

The wise man kept forcing him to eat, and then he ran him. For hours he whipped the poor man and made him run. Finally, at nightfall, full of rotten apples, fatigued, bleeding, he fell and vomited everything, the good and the bad, the apples and the snake.

When he saw that ugly snake come out of himself, he fell on his knees before his assailant.

"Are you Gabriel? Are you God? I bless the moment you first noticed me. I was dead and didn't know it. You've given me a new life. Everything I've said to you was stupid! I didn't know."

"If I had explained what I was doing, you might have panicked and died of fear," the holy one said.

"Muhammad has said, 'If I described the enemy that lives inside men, even the most courageous would be paralyzed. No one would go out, or do any work. No one would pray or fast, and all power to change would fade from human beings.'"

The holy man continued, "So I kept quiet while I was beating you, that like David I might shape iron, so that, impossibly, I might put feathers back into a bird's wing.

"God's silence is necessary, because of humankind's faintheartedness. If I had told you about the snake, you wouldn't have been able to eat, and if you hadn't eaten, you wouldn't have vomited.

"I saw your condition and drove my donkey hard into the middle of it, saying always under my breath, 'Lord, make it easy on him.' I wasn't permitted to tell you, and I wasn't permitted to stop beating you!"

The healed man, still kneeling, "I have no way to thank you for the quickness of your wisdom and the strength of your guidance. God will thank you."

— Rumi

When Everything
Goes Wrong

Go ahead, light your candles and burn your incense and ring your bells and call out to God, but watch out, because God will come, and He will put you on His Anvil and fire up His Forge and beat you and beat you until He turns brass into Pure Gold.

—Sant Keshavadas

The above quote may sound a little scary, but if you take it in deeply, it also may provide some comfort. Don't you and I often feel just beaten all to hell by our constant struggles, by the unwanted situations or annoying people in our lives?

We may feel bruised, defeated, exhausted, but then we remember, *maybe this what it feels like to be beaten and beaten until I am pure gold.* This is the faith I've been referring to.

So often we misunderstand faith by a mile. We create a so-called faith which is more like a letter to Santa Claus for everything we want. Then when we don't get it, we "lose our faith."

18

Sita and I, along with a few members of our staff at Human Kindness Foundation, once spent a day on the North Carolina death row unit, in Raleigh. I gave a couple of talks and we were able to spend some time hanging out with the condemned men.

One of them approached me to express his appreciation for our visit, and to share his glad tidings that Jesus has saved him. Now he knows that his next court appearance will go in his favor. He said Jesus will not allow him to be executed. He'll be sprung from prison; reunited with his family. Jesus won't let him down. The fellow beamed and said he has "complete faith."

An elderly woman wrote that she always had strong faith in God and was devoutly religious, but then she developed bladder cancer. Though she prayed, followed all the right regimens, and even traveled great distances to be blessed by holy sages, God did not fulfill her expectations. Her faith was shattered.

Does Jesus not love our condemned friend if the court upholds his execution? Is God ignoring the prayers of the elderly woman if she dies of cancer?

Better Catch Up On Religious History

If we take even a brief look at the history of the great world religions, it becomes clear that every genuine spiritual path has more to do with our response to things going wrong than with our problems being magically corrected.

Faith is a profound acceptance of life's Ultimate Goodness no matter what happens. It's a willingness on our part to accept *any* immediate situation — execution, cancer, loss, betrayal — as part of God's power and Grace and Love for us.

One of the great Sikh warrior-gurus was captured by the invading Mughal army. The enemy emperor was very excited to have finally defeated one of the pillars of the Sikh faith. He summoned his soldiers to bring the prisoner to him.

Bound in chains, the Sikh general was forced to his knees before the emperor. The emperor mocked him and said, "Let's see your great faith save you now!" The Sikh general calmly replied, "I can write down a magic formula which will shield me from all harm."

The emperor was furious, and shouted, "Bring this lunatic a paper and pen!"

The Sikh general wrote a few words, folded the paper and kept it in his hand. The emperor said, "Now, cut off his head!" A soldier raised his sharp sword, cut off the Sikh's head, and his body fell lifeless to the ground.

The paper was taken from his hand and read aloud: "You can have my head, but not my Faith."

The Holy Ones of every religion came here to show us the way that a person of faith can respond, not to a world which supports or rewards our faith, but to a world which often despises, condemns, rejects, exiles, tortures or even murders us for it.

Jesus didn't come to get us off of death row, heal our cancer or get us out of debt. He came to inspire the courage in us to live a Sacred Life as He did — to love others and dedicate our lives to the common good.

Faith in such a way of life is a very radical choice, because it is opposite to nearly everything we have been taught. It is extremely unpopular, too. He got crucified for it. So did many of his apostles and disciples through the centuries.

But if we make that choice and stick to it, we will touch something so incomprehensibly perfect and loving and wonderful that, believe it or not, it no longer matters so much whether we get our heads chopped off or spend the rest of our days behind bars. Once we touch that Love, the rest is small potatoes.

Saint Stephen touched that Love, and it was so fulfilling that even as an angry mob stoned him to death shouting "Blasphemer!!", all he could cry out was, "Father, please don't hold this against them." Imagine such Love!

Mahatma Gandhi touched that Love. As an assassin's bullets tore into his chest, his immediate response was, "Jai Ram!" which means "Hail God."

It Doesn't Always End So Badly

When the Chinese invaded Tibet in the 1950s, they killed countless peaceful monks and destroyed most of the monasteries. One Chinese general was especially known for his barbaric cruelty of disemboweling monks with his sword while they screamed for mercy.

At one remote monastery, word came that this particular general and his band of soldiers were on their way. All the monks fled to the hills except one elderly monk who sat calmly in the main hall.

When the general arrived and heard that one monk had not run in fear, he was enraged. He threw open the doors of the great hall, strode over to the small man and

> screamed, "DO YOU KNOW WHO I AM??! WHY, I
> COULD TAKE MY SWORD AT THIS VERY MOMENT,
> PLUNGE IT INTO YOUR BELLY AND REMOVE YOUR
> ORGANS WITHOUT BATTING AN EYE!!"
>
> The elderly monk looked into the general's eyes and
> softly replied, "But do you know who I am? Why, I could
> allow you to take your sword at this very moment,
> plunge it into my belly and remove my organs, without
> batting an eye."
>
> The general meekly lowered his eyes, bowed, backed
> away, and ordered his troops to leave the monastery at
> once.

So it's not that things always turn out badly. Indeed, every religion is full of such stories about the incredible power of pure faith. Faith has indeed healed the sick, raised the dead, parted the seas, moved mountains.

But it's a serious mistake to think that a positive outcome is the point. That's not the point of faith. It never has been. Those are just *demonstrations* of the Power and Glory we're dealing with — not guarantees. The elderly monk in the story above was telling the truth: He really would have been just as calm and fearless if the general had indeed disemboweled him. His faith was not tied to a particular result. He knew it was small potatoes.

Miracle stories serve to remind us that if God wanted our problems to be miraculously solved, they would be. So if the court says, "Execute him," or the doctor says, "Sorry, ma'am, but you're not responding to treatment," or Pontius Pilate says, "Crucify Him," then we know that God had the power to change it and didn't. So we can walk calmly, even through the valley of the shadow of death, knowing "Thou art with me." No bitterness, no doubts, no panic.

When Jesus left His disciples the final time and said, "Take courage and be of good cheer, for I am with you always," don't forget that He was speaking to a group of men who would be imprisoned, despised, killed. Jesus knew that, yet said, "Be of good cheer."

God's Power, Our Power

The issue is surely not one of power. Jesus has the power to save our death-row friend from execution, just as He had the power to spare Himself from the indignities and abuses He suffered at Calvary, or to pave an easier way for His apostles. Yet He didn't use His power to do so. And of course God can cure cancer, and sometimes does. But not usually. Jesus didn't heal *all* the lame; He didn't give sight to *all* the blind; He didn't raise *all* the dead.

A friend of mine was once suffering from kidney stones. One night when he was in unbearable pain, he cried out to Jesus, "Jesus, take this pain, please," and was startled to hear in response, "But I just *gave* it to you."

God's power designs and creates unlimited possibilities; *our* power is to bring the best of those possibilities to life in the world instead of the worst.

Look around at the world. People say, "Why does God allow children to starve? Why does God allow innocent people to be murdered? Why does God allow so many wars?"

But God has merely created all possibilities, including the elements necessary for a miserable world or a wonderful world. We have the free will to use those elements in a way which will bring more peace or more suffering. That's our choice, yours and mine, all the time.

We continue to choose anger over Love, fear over Love, national boundaries over Love, greed over Love, race over Love, self-protection over Love. God has given us free will so that we can make such choices. If we don't like the way the world is going, then we can begin to choose differently right now. Today. Right here! Waiting for everyone else to change first is a fool's game. Waiting for others to love us first, before we are willing to love them, is a fool's game.

> Divine Master, grant that I may not so much seek to be
> consoled, as to console;
> To be understood, as to understand;
> To be loved, as to love... ."

— Saint Francis of Assisi

How much we are loved by others is often outside our power. But what is within our power is our choice to love others. On the cross, hated and mocked, Jesus chose to say, "Father, forgive them, they know not what they do."

He loved them. He showed us the Way. He provided an example of following the advice of the Buddha: Focus on your ability to love, not your demand to receive it. Very often our immediate environments or circumstances are not under our control, but our choice of Faith and Love always is.

We will not be judged by what others did to us, but by how we responded.

Worldly Failure, Spiritual Success

Success is a series of glorious defeats

— Mahatma Gandhi

F rom the eyes of the Spirit, it is never too late to turn things around. And once we do, we will see that all those very things we considered to be our worst failures turn out to have been the very building blocks of our compassion and humility.

Many of us consider large parts of our lives to be miserable failures. Great! We're halfway there. We're "poor in Spirit." *Blessed are the poor in Spirit, for theirs is the Kingdom of Heaven.*

I love the story of Simon Peter in the New Testament. He was the boldest, the bravest, the most macho of all Jesus' disciples. When Jesus asked all the apostles, "How do you see me?," Peter was the only one who had the guts to say, "I see you as the Messiah, the Son of the Living God." Peter was a no-nonsense kind of guy. But he wasn't humble. He hadn't failed enough yet. He thought he was tough.

In the Garden of Gethsemane, Jesus hinted that there would be some trouble. Peter's response: "Well, even if the others run away, *I* will never leave you, Lord; *I* will never betray you." Jesus said, "Oh, Peter, you're just like all the rest." Peter's reply: "No way, Lord. I will not betray you. I would give my life for you!" Jesus said, "Peter, before the cock crows tomorrow morning, you will deny three times that you ever even knew me." No way. Not Peter. Tough guy. Righteous con. Not a coward. *Jesus is wrong this time. I'll prove it to him.*

We all know how it turned out, but have you ever thought about why? And why would Jesus then make that very same coward the Rock of the Church for all time to come? He ran away. He lied. He chickened out. He betrayed Him. **He failed miserably to be a decent human being. And that is precisely what finally made Peter ready to be the rock of the church.**

The one quality Peter lacked was humility. He thought he was better than all the rest, better than you and me. How then could he lead us to salvation? So, Peter's most miserable worldly failure led to his greatest spiritual success. His pride was humbled. That's what it took.

You and I have failed many times. We have let people down. We have been cowards, cheats, liars. We have hurt ourselves and others. If we allow our failures to open us up instead of shut us down, if we allow them to humble us instead of defeat us, then every lousy thing we have ever done can be turned into the very foundation of our devotion and compassion.

> "...I say to you that even as the holy and the righteous cannot rise beyond that which is in each of you,
>
> So the wicked and the weak cannot fall lower than the lowest which is in you also."
>
> — Kahlil Gibran, *The Prophet*

Do you "free-worlders" think you are better than a convict? Do you convicts think you are better than a snitch? Do you snitches think you are better than a baby-raper? Then you haven't failed enough yet. We are not better than anyone. That's the message. We have no right to look down on anyone, no matter what they have done.

Every human being contains the highest of the high and the lowest of the low. Peter had to find it out the hard way. I hope you and I don't. Peter must have been so ashamed and humiliated, he probably never wanted to show his face again. But he did. He came down from his lofty perch. He didn't quit or run away. He didn't try to forget all about it. He accepted his flawed nature, opened his heart and moved forward a quieter, gentler man who knew he indeed was "just like all the rest." He could then become the saint we are all destined to become.

Putting our Failures to Good Use

Without Peter's failure, there may not have been a Christian church. Without my failures, there certainly wouldn't have been a Human Kindness Foundation, no *We're All Doing Time*. Without your failures, you may not have the credibility to help some of the young kids in your neighborhood or cellblock to find a more decent way of life than the craziness that's all around them.

So the question is, are you using your failures yet? **Are you getting the spiritual point of your failures, and moving into a Sacred Life, devoted to faith, kindness and helping others?**

You and I deal with many people every day. Every one of those people hopes we are kind and humble and unselfish. They don't care where we learned it. They don't care whether it came easy or hard, through failures or successes. If the guy next to you starts choking,

27

he doesn't care where or how you learned the Heimlich Maneuver. He just hopes you use it!

One thing you can begin taking for granted is that every person you meet who seems to have courage, dignity, compassion and humility, has experienced failure and weakness and shame. So don't be an egomaniac and feel like you're the only one, or you're a worse one than the next. Everybody's got that stuff. Our spiritual victory rests only on what we are willing to do with it.

Faith and Failure

So now we can begin to see the connection between faith and failure. Our death-row friend and the elderly lady with cancer from the previous chapter express a type of faith which is tied to getting a particular result. Peter the Apostle had a faith which seemed to be as much in himself as in Christ. Both kinds of faith can lead us into failure because they are limited. We can then "lose our faith" as the elderly woman did, or we can allow that failure to lead us into a deeper, humbler faith in the Glory and Mercy of God, as did Peter. The choice is in our hands.

The Fortress of Anger

Anger comes to us because we lose contact with God. When we keep in constant contact with God, there is no room to be angry.

— Swami Ramdas

One thing that often comes from a misunderstanding of faith is a lot of anger. My elderly friend with bladder cancer became angry with God when she wasn't cured. Anger, from whatever source, can have a very powerful grip on us, and so it can be very useful to look at your relationship to anger, and begin to free yourself from its hold.

Much of the modern psychological advice about anger recognizes only two options: repression and expression. Since repression can be such a harmful and unhealthy way to deal with things, many people say the expression of anger is "healthy."

But spiritual teachings hold repression and expression as being somewhat alike. In both cases, we're caught in a dangerous, self-destructive illusion. There is a third way, which is to identify the roots of anger, and actually dismantle them.

Something I had noticed in my own spiritual work was that I would lose my temper less often, and at fewer people. That makes sense, right? However, the confusing part was that when I *did* lose my temper, the anger was just as intense or even more intense than ever! Also, the only people I would blow up at were the people I loved the most — Sita, Josh; I even screamed at my mother once, just a half hour before giving a church service on inner peace! I was so ashamed.

Isn't that strange? If meditation and prayer and clean living were whittling away the fury and rage inside of me, why wouldn't the *intensity* of anger decline along with the frequency? And why wouldn't my sweet little family be the first ones off the hook, instead of the *last* ones to enjoy my spiritual growth?

Nowhere to Hide

One of the blessings of regular spiritual practice is that it affords an opportunity to look closely at the best and worst parts of ourselves. That's what happened to me concerning anger in the middle of a two-month retreat of silence and partial fasting.

I fell into a period of horrifying anger that shook me to my roots, especially since I couldn't scream, shout, punch the wall, etc. I had to sit with it in silence. Imagine being angrier than you have ever been in your life and having nowhere to go with it except inside yourself.

Sitting all day, with no distractions, you can't possibly repress or push away anything; you can't turn on the TV or stuff your face or call a friend or go for a walk. It's just you and anger, right there in the moment of truth. Actually, I did lose control and break silence briefly, and then the anger toward myself *tripled* because I had broken my vow of silence. I fell sobbing on the floor, hating myself, hating my life, hating my confusion at what to do next — so much anger and self-hatred. So much *self*!

Anger Proves Love?

Still feeling adrenaline throughout my body, shame and despair in my heart, confusion in my mind, I prayed, "Please, let me see the truth, let me see where this comes from, even if I don't like what I see. May I see the truth of anger."

An image appeared — I was being comforted by my mother when I was a small child, apparently after she had lost her temper with me. I was shaking and crying, and she was saying, "Come on now, you know I love you! That's why I *get* so angry, because I love you so much." And then, as if on a movie marquee, I saw that I was learning, "ANGER PROVES LOVE."

Another image appeared: this time it was my whole family — all of us with bad tempers — sitting around making excuses about being "passionate" people, and actually putting down families that were calm and didn't scream at each other. Again, like a neon sign I saw,

ANGER = PASSION,
PASSIONATE = ATTRACTIVE / EXCITING,
UNPASSIONATE = DULL / BORING.

I began to grasp how many layers of innocently false notions, excuses and habit patterns underlie our emotional problems. We live according to how we see the world; we see the world to a large degree according to how we were taught. There is no one to blame, but there is a great deal to be corrected.

Looking honestly at my own heart, at my wounds from a lifetime of justifying anger, I said, "I no longer believe in this philosophy which my father was taught as a child, which my mother was taught as a child, which I was taught as a child. I no longer believe that anger proves love. I no longer believe it makes me a more interesting person. I believe it's a form of violence for me to rant and rave. I believe anger never helps. **Please, dear God, allow me to give up anger, as my contribution toward a more peaceful world.**"

I sat silently a while, and received various insights, teachings, about anger — for example, that anger is not a genuine emotion; it's a distraction. Anger is a smokescreen which takes us away from facing an uncomfortable truth. Many of us use anger to cover up embarrassment. Being angry is easier than admitting that our ego feels threatened or humiliated. Anger directs the attention to another person, or to a convenient enemy like the government, or cops, or criminals — anywhere but ourselves.

Much like sexual orgasm, *heavy* anger is so totally absorbing, it's almost impossible to see through the illusion while we are in it. Some of you reading this have given up precious years of your life because of anger; some of you are on death row because of anger. That's how tragically captivating it can be.

But I'm Right!

> If we use anger at injustice as the source for our energy, we may do something harmful, something that we will later regret. ...Compassion is the only source of energy that is useful and safe. With compassion, your energy is born from insight; it is not blind energy..
>
> — Thich Nhat Hanh

Probably the *most* difficult type of anger to let go of is what might be called Self-Righteous Anger: When someone else is absolutely, totally **Wrong** and we are absolutely, totally **Right!!!** Or, when someone we care about is hurting themselves, and WE'VE GOT TO MAKE THEM SEE THE TRUTH!!!

You know what I'm talking about, don't you? Rising up like Jesus with the money changers at the temple, we imagine, "This isn't 'my' anger! This is the Wrath of God at such a terrible injustice!" The problem is, Jesus' motivation was indeed "Righteous," but that is a world apart from "*Self*-Righteous Anger" — the key word there being *Self*.

A saint's anger has no ego in it, no personal fears or desires, no neurotic buttons being pushed; it's not self-protective like our anger, it's more like a hurricane or tornado — its awesome power isn't "against" us; it's just a mighty force of nature which humbles us and reminds us of our place in God's creation.

Righteous anger humbles us, but *self*-righteous anger seeks to defeat. There's a world of difference. Most of us have a long way to go before we can entertain the idea of expressing anger as a positive force in the world. As long as there's a "self," as long as there's someone wondering "Is anger okay?," then it's wise to consider it a dangerous form of expression.

Do You Want to Let it Go?

In the years since the revelation about anger, I've had a chance to feel how big an effect it had on me. I'd love to say I've never gotten angry again and never will, but that's not usually how these things work. Besides whatever else it is, anger is partly a habit, and habits usually take time — and practice — to change.

This can be a serious problem for people who experience being born-again or the raising of the kundalini or oneness with God, etc. — the ego-mind rushes to proclaim sweeping changes like, "I'll never be selfish again," or "I'll never get angry again," or "I'll never desire another cigarette." Then, when the old habit pops up a few weeks later, they get terribly depressed because they think their wonderful experience must have been false. The experience may have been genuine, but when the experience is over, that's when personal spiritual practice begins (check out Practice #10 on page 167 for one method of working specifically with anger).

> Bearing insult and injury is the highest practice. One has to experience unjustified harm, and then attempt to endure it without anger to know how nearly impossible it is to do so. It is then that one will realize that bearing is not just an ordinary practice, but truly the highest, because one has to be willing to let go of one's ego. And letting go of one's ego is the last practice before salvation.
>
> — Swami Sivananda

Sometimes when I feel anger coming on, I will sit down and try to see where I'm still holding *any* belief that anger is either real or justified. I'll find a tiny part of myself saying, "Listen man, you'd better hold on to a *little* bit of anger in such a vicious world! Gotta protect yourself, you know!" So I'll sit and look honestly at that, and remind myself, "**I no longer believe I *need* anger; I no longer believe anger protects me.**"

We begin to see that the things we pray to be rid of, we're the only ones holding on to in the first place. There's some belief *somewhere* inside of us that still feels we're safer with it, no matter how much suffering it has caused. It's like an abused wife staying with her violent husband rather than facing life alone.

With one hand I prayed to let go of anger, yet with the other, I held on to a *teensy* bit of it for emergencies, for a false sense of security. The way God responded to my prayers was not to remove the problem, but simply to let me see more clearly how I alone continued to be responsible for it — and how it must be my own choice to give up anger, not a magic trick on the part of God. We have to change false beliefs to let the new ones sink in.

It's amazing how reluctant or even terrified we are of accepting how peaceful life can be — while seeming to spend all our time seeking for it to be so. Every one of us embodies the Sacred One.

The best reason to move beyond anger is simply because it's beneath our dignity. Anger, hatred, revenge, greed, arrogance, addictions, fears, lusts — all are unworthy of us. We are Divine. We are Loved and we are Love. If we act accordingly, we find profound peace and freedom. If we keep fighting it, we never cease to do time.

It's Not the Top,
It's the Climb

From time to time, students of budo [martial arts] wonder if the large amount of time they are putting into their practice is worth what they are "getting out of it." While this seems to be a reasonable question, it actually reveals a fundamental lack of understanding. The time that one puts into the practice of an art *is* what one is getting out of it. It is the *process* of training that is truly valuable, not some eventual goal. All of life truly exists only at this instant.

— H.E. Davey

I n the mid '80's, when my son Josh was fourteen, I was asked to accompany a small group of kids from his school on an Outward Bound wilderness training course. I had heard a lot about how great those courses were, so I jumped at the opportunity to do one for free.

Off we went to the mountains of North Carolina for five days of ropes courses, rock climbing, rappelling down cliffs, and backpacking.

I've always seen that Outward Bound experience as a good reflection of the spiritual journey.

For one thing, the events themselves — all the physical challenges — may be what demand your attention during the course, but they're virtually meaningless except as the ways by which you develop *inner* qualities. It's the same way in our lives — the daily, practical world may require all our attention, but it would be crazy to forget the spiritual purpose behind every situation we face.

Picture signing up for the Outward Bound course, then spending the whole time just trying to get out of the damn woods — not learning how to keep dry in the rain or use a compass; not taking advantage of the opportunities to build courage and let go of fear.

On the other hand, if I were to say, "I must develop courage," and then sit in a chair to think about courage, that's not going to accomplish much, either. But the ropes course — climbing a skinny rope ladder forty feet up a tree, then walking across a narrow, slippery log during a light drizzle, and then grabbing onto another rope to swing all the way down to the ground — gave me a lot of opportunity to look at fear and courage.

There's nothing very important or noble about climbing a tree or swinging down a rope. Who cares? How does that help the world? Yet *courage* definitely helps the world, and it can't be seen, heard or felt by itself. It's like trying to see a color: Color is real, isn't it? Yet we can never see it by itself. We can see red *paint*, black *pen*, blue *sky*, but we can never see pure redness, blackness or blueness by themselves.

Inward Bound

Our lives are *solely* a journey into our Divine Nature — Love, Godliness, holiness, however you want to say it. That's the important part, like courage at the ropes course or redness on a piece of paper. **Every person and situation in our lives is merely an "inward bound" ropes course or boulder or cliff, designed precisely to bring out the best in us.** So, what's the point of signing up for the course and then complaining that all the events are too hard?

Years from now, we may hardly remember the challenges or the objects of desire, fear, or anger that once may have seemed important enough to lie, cheat, steal or even kill over. All we will have at the end of our lives will be the inner qualities, bad *or* good, which those situations gave us an opportunity to develop.

To go even further, if you entertain the idea of reincarnation, in our *next* life we won't even remember a single event or person, even the most important ones — our husbands, wives, children, parents, best friends, worst enemies — yet we will *be* the sum total of the honesty or deceitfulness, compassion or selfishness, courage or cowardice, greed or generosity, lust, gratitude, anger, patience, we have developed.

> Good deeds done in life are your only shield when you
> must die and go alone... to another world.
>
> — *The Ramayana*

In other words, even if you serve forty years in prison in this life, you won't remember it in your next life. But you will *be* the product of how well or poorly you used your time.

"What's Up There?"

In the rock climbing event at Outward Bound, we were asked to climb a very sheer boulder about thirty feet high.

I remember looking at the top of the boulder while I was on the ground waiting for my turn. The handful of people who had made the climb were standing around the top, looking incredibly happy and radiant and exhilarated. What an easy (and frequent) mistake it is to think, **"Wow, they look so happy; there must be something really great on top of that boulder!"**

Of course, there was nothing spectacular at the top of the boulder. Those people were enjoying the rewards of a tough climb. But how many times in our lives do we forget that, and merely try to get to the top of that damn boulder by every other means *except* going through the same effort and risks the people at the top went through?

I caught myself doing that awhile back, in a conversation with one of my favorite spiritual elders, Father Murray Rogers, an Anglican priest who lived in India, Israel and China for many years. I had just returned from India, and we were talking about my meeting with His Holiness the Dalai Lama of Tibet. I said that His Holiness was probably the most profoundly simple, deeply happy person I have ever met. Father Murray's response was, "Yes, and just *imagine* the pain and struggle he must have endured in order to become so thoroughly happy." I was seeing the Dalai Lama at the top of the boulder, and Murray's response reminded me that it was the climb, the climb. What we see in saints is the result of a long, hard climb, not a lucky break or an avoidance of difficulty.

You and I have every opportunity to make that same climb. And, of course, we're all doing it all the time, whether we like it or not. It's just that we can climb with ignorance, fear, avoidance, denial,

39

complaining, whining, and so forth, or with excitement, gratitude, respectfulness, perseverance and rock-solid faith.

The purpose of spiritual practices is not to get to the top with less effort; we will each be called upon to expend *tremendous* effort — to forgive the unforgivable, bear the unbearable, surmount the insurmountable; we will be called upon to develop lovingkindness in response to ignorance, hatred, fear and persecution.

Anyone looking for an easy, painless way through life should burn this book immediately and run in the opposite direction of any *genuine* spiritual teaching.

The purpose of personal spiritual practice is to *remember* that life is basically an Outward Bound course: The top is entirely meaningless except for the proper climb up to it. If yours seems to be a very tough climb, you may find even more joy at the top. And everyone has a boulder to climb, believe me. The difference between spiritual seekers and others is simply the awareness or faith that the struggle is indeed worthwhile, and leads to the top. Imagine what a constant hassle life must be to somebody climbing a difficult boulder with no faith in the climb, the struggle, or the top.

As you look around and see most of the people in the world in that predicament, the best help you can offer is to recognize your oneness with all climbers, recognize the oneness of our boulder and the typical scrapes and bruises which befall us all, and then pay attention to your own climbing, always willing to lend a hand when called upon.

When others see your increasing freedom and happiness and say, "It must be great to be up there on top of that boulder," you can remind them that it's not the top which leads to happiness, it's the climb.

Nothing Personal

I looked at the jail that secluded me from men and it was no longer by its high wall that I was imprisoned; no, it was God who surrounded me. I walked under the branches of the tree in front of my cell but it was not the tree, I knew it was God. It was God whom I saw standing there and holding over me His shade.

Or I lay on the coarse blankets that were given me for a bed and felt the arms of God around me, the arms of my Friend and Lover...

It was not the magistrate whom I saw, it was God, it was God who was sitting there on the bench. I looked at the Prosecuting Counsel and it was not the Counsel for Prosecution that I saw; it was God.

— Sri Aurobindo

any years ago, before he died, my father-in-law said there was one thing I had told him in the 1960's which made him look at his life differently. I asked him what it was and he replied, "You told me not to

take my life so personally. That was the strangest thing anyone had ever said to me. But it affected me deeply."

The above description by Sri Aurobindo (imprisoned in the early 1900s for revolutionary activities against British rule in India) is the ultimate direct experience of not taking things personally. His description is not daydreaming or poetry or philosophy; it's as real and clear as seeing your own hand in front of your face. It's not something merely to believe in; we must understand that one day we will see with those same eyes.

Impersonal Love

Those of us who have had the good fortune to spend time in the presence of a holy man or holy woman, a true spiritual master of some sort, have had at least a glimmer of the experience of impersonal love.

On the one hand, the love of such people is immense and intense and incomparable; that's what draws us to them. Yet on the other hand, it is not in the least bit personal. You know that they love the next person just as intensely and totally as they love you, and the next one after that and the next one after that... Yet that doesn't diminish the love they feel toward you; not one bit.

The love we feel from a master is not because we are pretty or rich or smart or clever or good; it's not a love based on anything personal. Rather, it's an oceanic and impersonal love based on the Big Truth of the Universe: God alone exists. And God is Love. That's what they see in every direction: **It's all Love, and it's not personal.**

We are caught in our small identity, while they are seeing our Large Identity. We are concerned with getting what we want, avoiding what we fear, protecting our lives at all cost; while they simply love us whether we are dead or alive, happy or unhappy, addicted or not addicted, in prison or in the White House — these are all meaningless trivial details to that sort of Love.

The Holy Ones love because Love Alone Is. And they teach us that such Impersonal, Unconditional Love is the only kind of love which does not lead to endless suffering.

Impersonal Conflict

A noble Samurai warrior pledged to track down and kill the man who had murdered his master. He spent every waking moment for three years hunting his prey. To avenge his master's death was the most sacred duty to a Samurai. His life would be a failure if he did not do so.

Finally, after tracking him through cities and towns and far-flung ports, he cornered the killer in an alley. It was definitely the right man, there was no doubt about it. The Samurai drew his sword and prepared to fulfill his duty, when suddenly the murderer spat in his face.

The Samurai hesitated for a moment, then sheathed his sword and began to walk away, his head hung down in shame. The man was so shocked that he ran after the Samurai and said, "But wait; I am indeed the man you sought. Why did you not kill me?" The Samurai replied, "Because I got angry when you spat in my face."

When Aurobindo saw the jail and the prosecutor and judge as God, he was freed from the personal drama entirely. He was then acting in

43

a play written, produced and directed by God, and starring God as all the characters. That doesn't mean he passively accepted injustice or evil; quite the contrary. I'm sure he turned in a brilliant performance for his own defense. The play is not without purpose.

But like Jesus with Pontius Pilate, it no longer mattered to Aurobindo whether he personally was found guilty or not guilty. His defense was not to save his own skin, but rather it was to defend right versus wrong, oppression versus democracy. He didn't care whether he spent his life in prison or in a palace; he was already free, he would be much the same in either environment. So without personal fear of any consequences, he could be the very best champion of his cause. He was fighting for something larger than himself.

If you have ever watched a true martial arts master (not the movie guys) in action, then you must have noticed how impersonal their behavior was. They are calm like scientists, focused like meditation masters, and free from the clutches of anger or fear.

The bulk of training in martial arts is to move beyond personal anger and fear in order to heighten one's powers of attentiveness and gracefulness. It is never another person whom you are attacking or defending against, but rather you are taking a stand against aggression and hostility.

That's why every genuine martial art stresses peacemaking first and physical conflict as a very last resort. No true martial artist is anxious to harm or humiliate another human being if it can possibly be avoided.

Violence is never used in service of a personal grudge, but only to defend the weak or uphold order and justice.

It's a hard teaching to explain — that life is not really about "us." It's not about people and events, as we think it is. It's actually about

Divine Principles being played out on the *stage* of people and events. As people and events, we are essentially meaningless — "Life's a bitch and then you die."

But as agents of the Divine, as characters in the never-ending "Play of God," we are heroes and heroines grappling with good and evil, loss and gain, pleasure and pain, hope and despair, compassion and apathy, generosity and greed, perseverance and laziness, courage and cowardice, love and hatred — the classic, universal forces which naturally oppose each other in each of us and in the universe as a whole.

The Boy Who Cried "Pickle!"

The only thing we know of historical figures, biblical figures, ancient martyrs and tyrants, is what they stood for. We don't know what their voices sounded like or their favorite color or whether they had bad breath, because our interest in them is not personal. All that's relevant for us are the principles they lived and died for; the inspiration or lessons they left behind.

The story of Daniel in the lions' den is not meant to teach us about a man named Daniel, but rather about the power of faith. **When our parents tell us about the boy who cried wolf, it's to emphasize the consequences of lying, not to tell us about a tragedy involving a boy and a wolf.**

The characters are not important, just the principles. The same thing applies to the events. If it had been Daniel in the wolves' den and the boy who cried lion, would it make any difference?

We have a very short life span, really we do. As Shakespeare put it in *MacBeth*,

> Life is but a walking shadow, a poor player
> That struts and frets his hour upon the stage
> And then is heard no more.

Yet we put all our attention on personal concerns and on an endless chain of specific events which are no more important in themselves than whether the boy cried, "wolf", or "lion", or "pickle." Our lives are about sacred principles, just like the lives of the characters in those stories.

We are given moment-by-moment opportunities to choose well or poorly. Choosing well, according to the saints and sages of all religions, is to choose the unselfish, the compassionate, the merciful and generous. Choosing poorly is to choose the selfish, the fearful, the vengeful, the greedy. It doesn't matter what our excuses are or what others have done to us. If you choose well, you represent the best of the sacred principles; if you choose poorly, you represent the worst of them.

> All suffering comes from cherishing ourselves.
> All happiness comes from cherishing others.

> — Tibetan saying

We are put here to love, respect and help each other. If we love, respect and help each other, we experience the connectedness between us and we touch the deeper meaning of life. If we don't love, respect and help each other, but instead get lost in fending for ourselves, protecting ourselves, acquiring riches for ourselves, etc., then we miss the point of being born, we miss the meaning and purpose of life by a mile. It's not personal. It's just the way we are designed.

Every religion tells us in one way or another that "The Word becomes flesh." But we, the flesh, become the Word as well. That's what happens when we are enlightened. It is a constant loop of the Word becoming flesh and the flesh becoming Word endlessly. Nobody home but God; no ego-self experiencing fear and selfishness; nothing going on but the Sacred being conscious of being Sacred, of existing simultaneously as formlessness and form; Word and flesh; Divine Love and Human Compassion.

Impersonal First

"This is the teaching of India:

A God not only impersonal, but personal also — Personal more perfectly, because Impersonal *first.*"

— Swami Kriyananda

A friend once asked, "You, Sita and Josh have such a loving family life. What's the secret?"

My response was, "All three of us love the spiritual path more than we love each other." Even as it came out of my mouth, I could hear how awful that sounded in our contemporary culture. Wasn't I supposed to say that we love each other more than anything else? But the truth is that the small, personal love is forever lacking unless the Big Love is the priority.

Loving God, truth, The Path, *the most*, is what gives a proper context to the love we have for each other. Without that context, personal love can be a road to Hell. "Baby, I love you more than anything. I would do anything for you. I can't think about anyone or anything else in the world!" Watch out if you hear that. Better run for cover when you start disappointing that person.

That sort of love never ends well. It always ends, but not well. It is emotion without intelligence. Personal before the impersonal.

Our lives must be about something bigger than the emotional self. Jesus said, "Seek ye *first* the Kingdom of Heaven, and everything else will be provided." In other words, recognize the biggest, loftiest, eternal principles first, then, like Sri Aurobindo, play your part with gusto.

Be as quick to defend the rights of a stranger as you would a member of your family. It's the rights you're defending, not the person. Be generous to the poor, whether you know them or not. It's mercy you're expressing, not personal affection. Forgive those who have wronged you, not because they deserve it, but because forgiveness is on the side of the saints, while grudges and vengeance bring the world one step closer to destruction. Take sides constantly with what is highest, noblest and good. Then see what happens.

Impersonal Personal Practice

And this is always the central purpose of personal spiritual practice: To be clear-minded and courageous enough to uphold what is right and good. It's often hard to tell the difference between right and wrong. If our minds are fogged by drugs or alcohol or lust or anger, then it's virtually impossible. We stumble around in confusion, and even when we try to do good, most often we're like a bull in a china shop, blundering about wrecking things.

To choose well, we must live well. We must respect our minds, bodies, and spirit. Self-discipline is essential. True tolerance and goodwill are essential. These qualities don't come about by reading a book. We must devote ourselves to spiritual practice, living simply, and doing good works (service). **We must take care of ourselves, not for selfish reasons, but simply because if we're not in good shape we won't be very helpful to others either.**

It's not personal. It's much bigger than that. Each of us is the full repository of good and evil, each of us is the hero of God's divine drama being enacted on Earth, each of us is creating the future of the world with each decision we make.

The Hesitation

Hanjiro Sensei was once passing through the countryside when he came upon a scene in which a 13-year-old boy and the 4-year-old child he had been carrying on his back had both fallen into the river and were about to drown. Everyone was in a panic and nobody knew what to do. Sensei quickly hiked up his *hakama* [traditional formal pants worn by samurai warriors] and tucked his leather-soled sandals into his belt. Then he jumped into the river and rescued the children.

The parents of the children were overjoyed when he returned them safely to the shore. As thanks for his courageous deed, they offered him a great basket filled with eggplants, gourds and watermelons. They said, "Please accept these as but a poor token of our gratitude. It is not much, but we are simple farmers and it is all we have at the moment. We certainly intend to call upon you again to thank you more appropriately."

But Hanjiro Sensei handed the basket back and replied, "You are most kind, but I am afraid I cannot accept such gifts."

The couple bowed their heads in shame and began to apologize for giving offense with such poor fare, but Hanjiro Sensei stopped them short, saying: "No, you have misunderstood my intentions. Your gifts are very much appreciated and I did not mean to offend by my refusal. What I meant was that, while I did rescue your children from the river, I am ashamed of the way I went about it.

"Before running into the river, I stopped to pull up my hakama and secure my sandals in my belt. If they had been my own children, I would not have wasted time with such petty preparations. I am deeply ashamed that I allowed this hesitation, as if your children were not as important as my own.

"That is why I am ashamed to receive your thanks and these fine gifts. Still, I would not want to compound the wrong by belittling your intention of gratitude, so with your leave I will accept a few small eggplants."

Hanjiro Sensei returned the rest of the gifts and went on his way, leaving all the farmers deeply moved.

"Buddha Time Off?"

Be there truly. Be one hundred percent of yourself in every moment of your daily life.

— Thich Nhat Hanh

A friend of mine is an American Buddhist teacher. One time, at a gathering of Western meditation teachers, he asked the Dalai Lama about a notion that is very popular in our culture. He said, "Your Holiness, how do you feel about the issue of needing to take time for ourselves? You know, our need to drop out of our roles and take time off, how do you feel about that?"

The Dalai Lama didn't understand the question, so he turned to his translator, who explained it a little more in Tibetan, but he still couldn't get it. So the fellow rephrased it about four different times, and finally the Dalai Lama got it. He burst out laughing and said, "Buddha time off? Bodhisattva time off? Ha ha ha!" What a concept!

A Living Buddha

Sita and I had the opportunity to visit the Dalai Lama at his home in India. The mountain village of Dharamsala is now home to thousands of Tibetan refugees who have fled the Chinese occupation of their country.

For those of you who don't know much about the Dalai Lama or the Tibetan situation, here's an extremely brief description: Tibet sits atop the majestic Himalayan Mountains between China and India. For many centuries, Tibetan life revolved mostly around studying and practicing the Buddha's deepest teachings under the guidance of their leader, the Dalai Lama.

Each time the Dalai Lama dies, he leaves clues as to where or when he will take birth again. Within a few years after his death, Tibet's sages also have dreams and visions which give further clues, and then they go in search of the new incarnation — the next Dalai Lama.

When the infant or toddler is found, he is tested in various ways, and when the sages are satisfied of his identity, the infant's parents gladly entrust him to a monastery, to be educated and trained by Tibet's wisest, most compassionate teachers, and groomed for his eventual role as leader of the Tibetan people.

Of course, being an incarnation of an enlightened master, the child often knows scriptures and teachings even before hearing them. Between such natural abilities and the extraordinary attention paid to his training, he becomes intelligent and insightful almost beyond imagination.

The current Dalai Lama can meditate for hours in profound peace, or discuss quantum physics with the world's most renowned scientists, or speak to the U.S. Congress about subtle details of foreign policy and human rights abuses. He has clearly transcended the chains and struggles of worldly life, yet chooses to remain fully involved in the world and 100% committed to relieving its suffering.

After centuries of peaceful spiritual living, Tibet was invaded by China in the 1950's. In 1959 — after years of trying to negotiate a peaceful settlement — the Dalai Lama was forced into exile. He and his advisors and family, like thousands of other Tibetans before and since, actually *walked* over the most rugged, snowbound mountain passes in the world, hiding from Chinese soldiers all the way. *Millions* of Tibetans have died, either victims of the Chinese army, or casualties of frostbite, avalanches and other hazards of their journey to freedom.

Sadly, this situation continues today. And although the Dalai Lama was awarded the Noble Peace Prize in 1989 for his dedication to the Tibetan cause, very few nations (including the U.S.) have lent any help at all, because China is so powerful and Tibet so obscure. So the struggle for Tibet's freedom continues.

Sacred Bagels

One of the most inspiring things about spending a week in Dharamsala was the *aliveness* of religious practice there. Most of the population are Buddhist monks and nuns, and the Dalai Lama is their one single, uncontested religious leader; he's alive, right there, preaching kindness and joy as the most important duties of life. So even just walking down the street in Dharamsala becomes a very happy experience, bowing almost constantly, exchanging greetings of lovingkindness with nearly everyone.

During our meeting with His Holiness, I put all my attention into being present, open and receptive in the presence of such a great spiritual elder. I tried to look very practically — "He's got two legs, two arms, a head, a nose. We both wake up in the morning, both go to sleep at night. What is the real functional difference between his experience and mine?"

One of the things I noticed is simply that he's "full-time." You and I may go to a church service or a spiritual retreat, and with enough mutual support and encouragement, we may let down our guard, and be willing to feel the Living Spirit with each other. We'll be open and trusting, experiencing the preciousness of being together and practicing together.

Then the service ends, and on the way home we stop for gas, or a bagel or something. And here is the difference: You and I are then willing to pretend with the gas station attendant, or with the cashier, that life *isn't* so sacred. We pretend that this is just buying a bagel, this is just getting gas. We won't look in their eyes. We won't be intimate. It's like an unspoken agreement to avoid feeling how precious we are to each other.

The Dalai Lama, and other saints like Mother Teresa and Gandhi, simply don't turn it off! They go into the station and see a Precious Child of God taking their Divine Credit Card for the Sacred Gas, and they don't hide it from that person taking the credit card! Their whole presence says, "It's all equally sacred." Getting gas, praying in church, buying a bagel, are all the same Mysterious Miracle. They live in Love, so of course they are in Love with the gas station attendant. And at the bagel shop, they'll be in Love with the bagel boy.

The Great Equalities

One of the things I love most about the spiritual journey is the humbling equality with which we are born. Regardless of wealth or race or culture or era, we are all born with several conditions *exactly* the same.

The first Great Equality is that the moment we are born, whether we are born in a crack house or the White House, we have no idea when or how we will die. Thank you. Thank you, God, for making us so equal. We have no idea whether we will live to be 2 years old or 105. The Greatest Humbler of all.

The second Great Equality is that we have no idea who or what the most important influences of our lives will be.

Looking back on the past, we may say, "Wow, little did I know when I woke up that one fateful morning, that was the day my life would change forever... ." It takes practice to realize every day of our lives, with every person we meet, *this could be the most important experience of my life.*

That attitude of perpetual openness is reflected in the core of both the Jewish and Christian traditions, of being ready *every moment* for the appearance of the Messiah — the instrument of our deepest salvation. It can come in any form, from joy or sorrow, success or failure, alone or with multitudes. We must therefore have *infinite respect* for the spiritual potential of all people and experiences.

The third Great Equality is our Common Tasks. One of the interesting ideas that has come up over the past 30 years in the West is, "I create my own reality." There is, of course, some truth in that. We surely create some of the mind-body attitudes which can lead to illness or health, but to take that idea into the realm of the deepest spiritual truths is childish. It misses the truth by a mile.

If you say, "I *choose* for my heart to digest food instead of pump blood," that's simply not going to work. There is a certain obedience and surrender required to natural and spiritual laws. The stomach digests food, the heart pumps blood, the lungs process air. Everybody is born with many equal physical responsibilities.

Well, everyone is born with a *spiritual* responsibility also, as specific and real as our heart's responsibility to pump blood: **We must learn to love one another, to receive and express goodness.** It doesn't matter whether we believe in it or not. Obey it and we will thrive, disobey it and we won't. Period.

Look all over the world and see the people who unselfishly receive and express goodness, who are *dedicated* to the cause of love. They're the only people who are truly happy. They have tapped into the one mysterious, wonderful connectedness that frees them to live full-time in love.

We Need Some Elders, and it's US...

After I came out of a long retreat, I looked around at my own culture. I saw the crises that we are in, the problems that exist in the American family. I see that on one hand, many of us have come a long way in order to be able to acknowledge Eastern masters, saints from other traditions.

But on the other hand, where are the American realized beings? Where are the enlightened elders who share our cultural experience; people who experience the bombardment of television commercials and fast-food restaurants, gang violence and hundred-million-dollar sports contracts?

The American realized beings will be people whose motivation is especially compassionate toward our unique situation of being brought up in a bizarre combination of unparalleled affluence amid vast spiritual loneliness and confusion. They will be people who come from the same place, yet have transformed entirely and died into the living spirit.

I started thinking, *I'll bet there are men and women in monasteries, convents, caves right now who are from the American culture and are just about ready to come out and say, "Here we are."* I thought, *All I have to do is make sure I can recognize them when they appear.*

But those thoughts didn't really cut it, because a little voice in me said, *Schmuck, you're it!* Me. You. Little old us. Because if it's not you and me, it's not us. Are we willing? Our people are so confused and dismayed, so fearful, jaded, and unhappy. Can we take that as inspiration and encouragement to get on with our awakening? What this country needs more than anything else is for us to become elders, walking the streets and doing our jobs. Really happy, classic, ageless spiritual human beings.

Sacred Practice, Sacred Living

What is it that turns us into a being whose very presence quietly and modestly evokes the best in others? How do we become someone who can remember the sacredness of life while buying a bagel and pumping gas? Practice. Sacred Practice. And then putting what we practice into expression. That's Sacred Living.

57

So, I hope you take this opportunity to decide what modest daily practice you're going to begin without further delay. The last section of this book is a collection of simple and powerful practices you can include in your daily schedule. There are lots of other sources for spiritual practices, including my book, *We're All Doing Time*.

Give yourself a chance to find out for yourself whether all of this is real or not. Be a daily practitioner for a month or two and see whether your life feels any different. It is never going to be fully convenient to begin. If you think you have to wait for something, you're missing the point, and you may well be waiting forever. *Now* is the only time we can ever use.

"NOW!"

I had just one desire — to give myself completely to God. So I headed for the monastery. An old monk asked me, "What is it you want?"

I said, "I just want to give myself completely to God."

I expected him to be gentle, fatherly, but he shouted at me, "NOW!" I was stunned. He shouted again, "NOW!" Then he reached for a club and came after me. I turned and ran. He kept coming after me, brandishing his club and shouting, "Now, Now."

That was years ago. He still follows me, wherever I go. Always that stick, always that, "NOW!"

— Theophane the Monk, *Tales of a Magic Monastery*

...How Little We Need

Half the confusion in the world comes
from not knowing how little we need.

— Richard Byrd

Simple Joy

Soon after the death of Rabbi Moshe of Kobryn, one of his disciples was asked, "What was the most important thing to your master?"

The disciple thought for a moment, and answered, "Whatever he happened to be doing at the moment."

— Martin Buber, *Tales of the Hasidim*

A friend of ours here in North Carolina recently lost her beautiful 19-year-old son to suicide. She told us he was the *sixth* among a small group of friends who have committed suicide in the past two-and-a-half years. Suicide is now the third leading cause of death among teenagers (murder is #2, car accidents #1).

We need to start asking ourselves some searching questions about why life seems to be of so little value to our kids. From a spiritual perspective, one sentence can sum up the whole thing — not only our own and our kids' problems, but our planetary problems too, from pollution to wars:

Human life is very deep, and our dominant modern lifestyle is not.

Life is deep, *we* are deep, and we're not acting like it. Life is inherently joyful, yet we're not enjoying it. We're caught in the details, which will count for nothing if we don't wake up to our spiritual depth.

Right now, while you are reading this, take a moment to center yourself in your body, in this place you sit, and feel yourself breathing, and smile. Don't just speed-read on to the next paragraph, please. Let go of past and future. Appreciate that you're alive; appreciate knowing how to read. Appreciate knowing about spiritual wisdom. Bring a soft smile of gratitude into your heart and onto your face.

This is what we rarely pass on to our kids. Our kids don't get the message from us that being alive feels good. We may say it to them occasionally, but how do we *show* it in our everyday activities? Even the best, most loving people often seem to be working themselves into the ground, keeping up a frantic pace just to pay the bills and to keep resolving each day's repairs, breakdowns, details and little crises.

Would YOU Want to Grow Up?

You must admit, from a kid's point of view, growing up doesn't look very appealing. Besides seeing so many joyless or downright angry adults in schools, businesses and government, it also must appear that being an adult means being powerless. Think about it: "Honey, I'd love to coach your soccer team this year, but I just can't. I'm sorry. I have to do such-and-such, I wish I didn't have to, but I do... ." How many times do our kids hear such stuff? What's the message they receive — that adult life, everyday life, is mostly a drag and out of control?

There is a great line in the movie *When Harry Met Sally* that can be a very good reminder to us all. In one scene, Meg Ryan is in a restaurant with Billy Crystal. She's trying to prove how easily men can be fooled by women faking orgasm, so she does a very convincing job of going into ecstasy over her food. She really gets into it, and attracts a lot of attention. The waitress then goes to the older woman at the next table and says, "Can I take your order?" and the woman says, "I'll have whatever she's having."

Now think about your own life. If there were an invisible child or teenager attached to your hip, following you throughout the day, would he see somebody who is really enjoying the moments of who she is and what she's doing? Would he see somebody who would inspire him to say, "Boy, I want what she's having," or "I can't wait to be a grown-up?" Would he see peace? Would he see a depth of joy and contentment, equanimity, a gracefulness about your life?

How many simple, peaceful, truly *happy* adults do our kids get to see? How many adults are deeply content with their lives and enjoy what they do? How many are happy about getting older, and unafraid of dying? How many are relaxed and calm, with time to play hooky from work every now and then in order to spend some unplanned, unstructured, unproductive time with their families, or participate in a cause they truly believe in?

Everyday Life Is All We've Got

The deep, wonderful secrets of life, the mysterious presence of the Divine, the joy of cherishing each other, the beauty of nature, the satisfaction of helping out, our journey into the Ageless Wisdom — all exist *only* in our everyday life. There is no bigger ball field on which to find meaning. It's either right here, today, or it's nowhere.

We seem to be knocking ourselves out in pursuit of a vague image of success or frenetic modes of recreation, while the real quality of our everyday life with our families and communities steadily declines. We're asleep at the wheel, swept up in a fitful, agitated dream, and we're missing some gorgeous scenery which only passes by once.

> When the Buddha experienced his great enlightenment, he got up from where he had been sitting and walked toward the village. The first person who saw him was awestruck by his radiance and power. The man approached him and said, "Sir, what are you? Are you a god?" The Buddha said, "No." The man said, "Well, are you a spirit or a demigod?" Again, the Buddha said, "No." "Are you a human being?" Once more, the Buddha said, "No." The man said, "Well what are you, then?" The Buddha replied, "I am awake."

Then the Buddha spent the rest of his life making it clear that all of us can awaken too. The joy is right here; we just need to wake up to it.

The basics of life are no different today than they were thousands of years ago: Get up in the morning, take reasonable care of our bodies, minds and souls; do some kind of work which benefits the world instead of harms it; respect and cherish each other, and then get some sleep. **It's important to keep our big view simple, and to pass such a simple view on to our kids.** They desperately need a Bigger View than television, malls, and the salaries of their favorite athletes and movie stars.

Koyaanisqatsi

So what has gotten so out of whack in modern times? Why does it seem so complex and draining merely to pay the bills and get by? For one thing, our consumer culture encourages us from the time we're born to have *ceaseless* desires.

To put it simply, we want so much, all the time, that we have not even noticed how much quality of life we have given up; how much peace of mind we have sacrificed; how much fun with our family we have forfeited, in order to have cellular phones, TV's in every room, new cars — all the stuff that counts for ZERO in the deeper part of ourselves, in our Kingdom of Heaven.

We used to think that a two-income family was a choice. How many Americans feel that it is a choice nowadays to have a two-income family? Many would say a two-income family is now required just to barely scrape by. Most of us are working much too hard.

> Americans have more time-saving devices and less time than any other group of people in the world.
>
> — Duncan Caldwell

Some statistics say that we currently have 30% less leisure time than our parents' generation, even with all our labor saving devices — which we labor mightily to uphold. We say, "The computer's really going to save me a lot of time" and then we're on the Internet all night, not taking good care of our health. Or we get a microwave oven because we don't have time to cook, so we end up buying unhealthy and expensive TV dinners to cook in it. Hopi language has a word for this kind of lifestyle: *Koyaanisqatsi*, which means "life out of balance."

American life especially has been about "keeping up with the Joneses," but it's time we noticed that the Joneses are not happy. One of their kids is on drugs, the parents are in divorce court, Mr. Jones is $50,000 in debt, and Mrs. Jones is taking anti-depressant medication. This is no joke; this is the reality of the American Dream for many people today. Time to wake up from such a bad dream.

"My Favorite Food"

We have seriously devalued being content. We say, "C'mon man, get motivated. Go do high-impact aerobics. You got your M.A.? Go get your Ph.D.!" We are constantly brainwashed to want and to be and to do. **If one of our kids says, "I'm really content," we start getting worried that they're not going to have enough "drive" to become successful.**

Every advertisement tells us, "Go, man go!" Nike says, "Just Do It!" There are billboards in Los Angeles that read: "You Can Rest When You're Dead." It's no wonder that we believe it after awhile. The whole consumer culture orientation makes us feel constant inadequacy because of all the temptations dangled in front of us; all the things that we could be, could do, could have. Or, as our culture implies, *should* be, *should* do, *should* have.

But when we take a look at any sacred text, or the advice of any saint or sage, it begins to dawn on us that they are all saying, "Dear Ones, it's here, now, or it never comes. It's here, now."

My favorite story of contentment comes from my son's experience as a volunteer in Guatemala. When he was 23, Josh spent time in a small Mayan community, and his Spanish tutor was a young Guatemalan woman about his age. He was in a fairly remote village, and they ate beans and tortillas twice a day, seven days a week. That was the diet.

66

Josh chatted with his tutor once about food; he asked her whether she had ever tasted pizza. She said yes, her family had been to Guatemala City a couple of times. He asked her about a few different foods, like pasta and hamburgers. "Yes, yes... ."

Then finally he asked the question that took him by surprise and deepened his life. He said, "If you could have any kind of food in the world, what would you have?" And she immediately said, "Beans and tortillas. That's my favorite food."

Now, can you imagine most American kids enjoying the same meal two nights in a row, let alone twice every day? We have the "freedom" to have Chinese food one night, Italian the next, Ethiopian after that. And yet, for all these varieties of the palate, are our kids really happy? Are they content?

This is a metaphor for our larger experience as well. For all the satisfaction that comes from this tremendous range of choices that we have, are we happy? Are we there yet? That young Guatemalan woman's simple response seriously deepened my son's understanding of contentment.

Ask Yourself This...

Here are some useful questions to ask: Every day, am I more contented? Do I have a quiet joy? Am I becoming a bigger, wider, deeper human being of peace and joy on a daily basis? Or am I feeling like it's right around the corner, and I have to just knock myself out for a few more days, weeks, months, years, and then some mythical day I'm going to open to my peace and joy?

These are the kind of questions that help us to step back and take a more objective look at our lives. **We have a great number of** options, yet sometimes we blindly follow something just because everybody else is going in that direction, or because it's easy, or because there is an immediate payoff. And I know from my own experience that peace starts now or it never starts; that contentedness is absolutely one of the most important qualities there is; and that these things are not opposed to a dynamic lifestyle in which we actively serve and contribute.

Living simply is possible. A joyful, contented life is our true nature. Life can be rich and rewarding; but we have to give up our constant demand for more, new, bigger, better... . It's literally killing us.

The Great Activism

Blow up your TV,
Throw away your paper,
Move to the country,
Build you a home.
Plant a little garden,
Eat a lot of peaches,
Try to find Jesus,
On your own.

—John Prine

Another related culprit of our imbalance, our *koyaanisqatsi*, is the role of "career" in our lives. Career seems to have become the accepted hub around which everything else revolves. We choose career over our own health. We choose career over our mates and children. We choose career over our time to study, pray, walk, hike, meditate, participate in community life. We fuss over our children's potential careers like it's the most important thing in the world. If our child wants to take a year or two off between high school and college, we freak out. We worry they'll "get behind." What does that mean? *Behind what?*

Career is not deep enough to be the center of life. It just isn't. Career is not who you are. It's something you do for twenty or thirty years and then you stop. If you sink all your identity into it, then your life hasn't started until your career begins, and it's basically over when your career ends. **One British study showed that men were almost *twice* as likely to die within the five years after they retire than if they had continued working!** That's sad, foolish and unnecessary. Career hardly scratches the surface of who you are.

"What do you do?" "Who cares?"

Sixty years ago, if you were to say to my grandfather, "So Ben, tell me, what do you do?" he would have looked at you quizzically and said, "I do a lot of things." If you persisted and said, "No, I mean, how do you make a living?" he would have probably said, "Why do you care?" It wasn't considered very important.

It's only *very* recently that people began associating their self-worth, self-esteem, status in the community, their very *identity*, with their career. It's just a passing fad in human history. Don't get caught up in it. My grandfather was considered a pillar of his synagogue and community — and what he did for a living was paint houses. My grand-uncle collected and sold rags. Both honorable, esteemed men.

To them, what they did for money was the pettiest part of life. No blue-collar/white-collar nonsense. So long as it was honest, who cared? **And further, they worked as *little* as possible, not as much.** They fed their families, paid the rent; they weren't trying to "get ahead" (another interesting expression. "Get ahead" of what?)

In other words, it was not always taken for granted that everyone was trying to become wealthy, move into a bigger house or buy their kids every little expensive gadget that came along.

Character and virtue and wisdom and joy are the mark of a person, not one's choice of career. Contentment is a virtue. A lack of materialistic ambition is not such a bad thing. Remember, *man does not live by bread alone.*

Bigger Ain't Always Better

The most valuable form of activism in this day and age may be to explore a lifestyle based around simple living and simple joy. It may take toning down our materialistic demands and figuring out how to live on less income, but that process itself will begin to save some of the world's resources and thereby address many of the world's pressing problems, as well as give us more time with our families and communities.

Most people think they can't get by on less. But the last time I looked around a typical suburban neighborhood of twenty houses, I realized that there were probably twenty lawnmowers, twenty computers, ten chainsaws, and a lot of other expensive contraptions which each family may only use a few days a month. Among those twenty families I saw about *forty-five* cars, costing a fortune in insurance, repair, registration, gas and so forth. Those twenty families may own fifty or more televisions.

That's not food and shelter; that's a wasteful modern lifestyle which we can change. We must think for ourselves and talk with friends and have the guts to try some things differently to take the pressure off. This is a fitting time to explore various old and new ways of living with others in intentional communities, co-housing, collective ownership of vehicles and tools, and other ways to cut down on the wasteful expense of modern living.

When I was growing up in the 1950's, few families had a television. So a bunch of us would gather at a neighbor's house to watch something — which of course, provided natural opportunities to socialize with the neighbors. This still goes on in many other countries. But in our society, TV has become the *opposite* force: Even poor families may have little TV's in several rooms, so we hardly even socialize with our own families, let alone our neighbors.

This is a strong example that more is not always better. In cultures where people must share limited resources — TV's, tools, vehicles — their sense of community is much stronger. We have accepted a model of progress and personal choice which has isolated us as individuals and actually damaged our family and community life a great deal. Is it really progress?

So these days, it is political activism to go against that tide and live more simply. Share the table saw with Ernie down the block. Cut down to one TV in your home (and cut down your use of it greatly). Eat meals with your family, go for walks, do daily readings of spiritual stories, occasionally play hooky together and go skip stones across a pond.

It is activism to explain to our kids the hype and deceit involved with the endless ads which incite them to buy something new or get in on the latest craze. Our kids may be deeper if we treat them with depth. Our kids may be deeper if we are. No guarantees, but they'll certainly have a better chance.

The Big, Eternal Activism

And of course, providing a *spiritual* perspective to our kids is always the Big Activism. **It horrifies me how many people proudly say,**

"I tell my kids they have to figure out whatever they want to believe in. That's their business."

My God, why would we put such a burden on our children? We help them to walk, talk, ride a bike, drive a car. But we don't teach them about their connection to the Great Wisdom handed down by so many elders and traditions? We don't teach them about the common threads of all religions?

If family life doesn't provide a deep view about our purpose for being alive and the importance of respecting all beings, then our children may grow up like in the story *Lord of the Flies* — which seems to be exactly what's happening for a great number of modern children: Lost, selfish, close-minded, angry, violent. Without lots of *joyful* guidance from us, they meet a confusing and frightening world.

I find it sweetly ironic that the Great Activism of our day — inspiring our children to stay alive, and to live and behave in civilized ways — requires us to rediscover the simple joy of life for ourselves as well. We have to do it. Nothing less will do.

Signs of the Times

If you don't feel ready for huge steps like co-ownership or slashing your salary in half, take small steps. Make one practical change this week which will allow you to live on a little bit less and be less burdened with possessions. Turn off the TV and spend a little more time in nature; find a service project that the family can do together, like helping an elderly neighbor winterize her home. There are more ideas in Practice #11 which begins on page 169. And read Practice #7 beginning on page 158 for a spiritual practice that the whole family can do together.

If you're in prison, ease up on the financial requests you make of your family. Become an example to your family of someone who knows that she doesn't need a bunch of "stuff" to be happy. Get involved in a service project like teaching illiterate inmates to read. Ask more questions about your family's daily lifestyle and see if you might provide some practical suggestions for taking the pressure off.

> When it is evening, you say, "It will be fair weather; for the sky is red." And in the morning, "It will be stormy today, for the sky is red and threatening." You know how to interpret the face of heaven, but can you not interpret the signs of the times?
>
> — Jesus

We need to see the signs and we do need to act, however modestly. We can turn ourselves and our kids around from this hectic joyless chaos toward a more civilized way of life, but it will take some conscious effort. Let's do our part.

The Ultimate Child

> "Oh where is that ultimate child, the child who is driving the entire world insane?" cried the Rabbi of Pscizche."
>
> Once in his youth, the Rabbi confronted a man who was totally immersed in his business ventures. "Why are you so totally absorbed in trying to make money? Why do you not devote more time to prayer and Torah study?" The man responded, "You see Rabbi, I really do not require that much to live on, but I must work to provide for my family, especially my *child* and his future."

Years went by and that child became a grown man. He, too, became engrossed in worldly pursuits. "Why do you not take time out to further your spiritual growth," the Rabbi of Pscizche asked of him. The man answered, "I cannot, Rabbi. For though I do not need much for myself, I must think of my child, and his future."

Then that child grows up, and the story repeats itself generation after generation. No one has adequate time to live according to his beliefs because everyone must provide for his child, and so on.

"Somewhere, then," the Rabbi exclaimed, "perhaps at the end of time, we will find that ultimate child, for whose welfare countless generations have so toiled that they've neglected their own values in the process. Where is that ultimate child? Is he not but a fiction? A non-existent end-point? An illusion that has driven the entire world into an insane striving toward futility?"

— Rabbi Abraham J. Twerski

Feasting on
Poisoned Cake

Would you like to save the world from the degradation and destruction it seems destined for? Then step away from shallow mass movements and quietly go to work on your own self-awareness.

— Lao Tzu, *Hua Hu Ching*

Perhaps the saddest, most disturbing "shallow mass movement" of our day is personal consumer debt. While on a flight to Nebraska to do some talks and workshops recently, I read a cover story in *USA Today* about the problem of personal debt. The average American is $10,000 in debt, mostly on credit cards. Most people pay the minimum monthly payment.

The article showed on a graph that with a debt of $10,000, paying the minimum of $200/month — which is a pretty big chunk of most people's salary — it would take *fifty years* to pay off the total. Fifty years. Is that okay with you?

Let's get specific. In his book *Life Without Debt*, Author Bob Hammond spells it out quite clearly.

> Need more furniture? If you buy $2000 worth of furnishings with a credit card charging 18.5% interest and pay off the balance by making minimum payments, it will take you more than eleven years to repay the debt. By the time the loan is paid off, you will have spent an extra $1,934 in interest alone — almost the actual cost of the furniture.

Almost $4000 for $2000 worth of furniture! Are you ready to pay two or three times what something is worth just because you want it *now*? Eleven years down the line, you probably won't even *have* that couch anymore, but you'll still be paying for it. That's the truth about credit.

Peddling credit cards to college students is also a big industry now. The article said modern students no longer want to live "on the cheap" while in school. No more old jalopies, mattresses on the floor, peanut butter sandwiches. Now, minimum monthly payments enable them to live in whatever style they like. But again, at what cost? Their whole lives? According to *The Boston Globe*, besides such credit debt, American college students also have an average debt of $18,000 in student loans upon graduation with a bachelor's degree, and *$40,000* average debt for masters' degrees or PhD's. One-third of all Medical school graduates owe more than $75,000!

Amazing. Millions of people, young and old — precious, divine vehicles of God — are rushing to enslave themselves to banks and other corporations for the rest of their lives, to support a lifestyle which has little to do with joy or truth or freedom. The credit card companies are offering free poisoned cake, and we are feasting on it by the truckful. Have we gone nuts?

What's the Alternative?

There is certainly an alternative to being consumer sheep fattened for the slaughter. We can, as Lao Tzu suggested, "step away from shallow mass movements" both internally, through personal spiritual practices which clear our vision and cultivate our courage and faith; and externally, through creating a simpler lifestyle which not only requires a lot less money, but also gives us more time for the things that really do matter. We can go from "loving things and using people," back to "loving people and using things."

It takes work, of course. Anytime we step aside from the crowds there will be work involved. There may be people trying to discourage us. Fellow slaves mocking our efforts to be free. Mahatma Gandhi called his autobiography, *The Story of My Experiment With Truth*. That is the opportunity each of us has. Not just what we read in the evening, not just in church on Sundays, but to make our everyday lives a grand, noble, good-humored, experiment in truth — where we live, what we do for a living, how our children are educated, the causes we embrace and support, how we spend our free time; all one thing. An undivided whole. A deliberate life. A rare thing in today's world.

Many people say, "Oh, I could easily live in a simpler way or dedicate my life to a cause I believe in, but it would be unfair to my children. What about health care? What about their college education? I don't want to limit their opportunities."

Raising our kids to be indentured servants of the credit card companies and prostitutes to the dollar seems extremely limiting to me! I know perfectly healthy people in their twenties taking jobs they don't like because the employers offer the most "bennies" —

benefits like health insurance and retirement plans. Do we want our kids to sell their lives to the highest bidder? Is that all life is about? We have seriously lost our "Big View."

Joyful Risks

The truth is, no matter how we live, we limit our children's experience. Poor kids think there are no bad parts to being rich; rich kids think there are no good parts to being poor. Kids on a farm don't know the benefits of traveling, and kids who have seen the world may miss out on having one place they can call home. Our personal interests and values necessarily define much about our children's lives, so we must make sure we have deliberate and deep values rather than the "default" values of a dysfunctional, unhappy culture.

I encourage you to try the suggestions in Practice #11 beginning on page 169. It's a great time in human history to take some joyful risks with our experiments in truth. We must begin reclaiming our sanity, dignity and true freedom before our kids become absolutely convinced that such words are foolish or old-fashioned.

Living in Tune
with Our Beliefs

If we divine a discrepancy between a man's words and his character, the whole impression of him becomes broken and painful.

— Charles H. Cooley

M y Guru, Neem Karoli Baba, used to say, "Life is really very simple; you just keep making it complicated." One clear example of that is the connection between our deepest beliefs and the way we live our everyday life. It's so simple — if our actions are in tune with our values, we'll feel good about ourselves and life will work as smoothly as it can. If we act contrary to what we believe in, we will gradually grow to hate ourselves, and life will be a constant and unfriendly struggle.

Of course, no one said it's *easy*; just simple. Even though I saw the top of that boulder in the Outward Bound course from the ground, I still had to spend a tremendous amount of energy to climb it. Self-respect requires self-discipline. Decency requires conscience and courage. Kindness requires forgiveness and patience. A good life happens to be a fair amount of work. It's not for the lazy. But it is a *simple* principle: **We all have beliefs and values. If we live by them we will thrive, if we don't, we will wilt.**

You may say, "I don't know what I believe in, I don't even know what you mean by my 'deepest values'." But if you don't know you've got a thousand dollars in your wallet, it doesn't mean you're broke. It just means you must learn to look through your wallet more thoroughly. Your heart is a wallet which holds deep values and vast riches; it isn't empty, I assure you. You may simply not have looked through it for a while. That's one important aspect of personal spiritual practice.

The Pit of Self-Hatred

There is a term for the gap that exists between our deepest beliefs and our daily behavior — it's called self-hatred.

If my heart believes it's wrong to steal, then in order to let myself steal something, I may close off a little part of the way I receive messages from my heart. If I believe in kindness, then in order to be cruel, I may close off another little part of my heart. If I believe in courage, then cowardice may close off another little part of my heart. And so it goes. If I don't know what I believe, then every day I'm probably closing off at least a few more parts of my heart by doing things that are easiest or selfish instead of what I may think is *right*.

By the time we're adults, we've closed off our hearts in so many ways, it's like a garden hose that's all kinked up, and the Water Of Life is hardly able to drip its way through. We lose all respect for ourselves because we don't feel our wonderful hearts, and eventually we become extremely stuck in self-hatred. We lose hope in real joy or happiness, and assume we have to settle for damage control and barely "getting by."

Does that sound familiar? Most of us pass through such a "dark night of the soul" at least once or twice; the trick is not to get stuck in it for our whole lives.

I was like that when I was a kid. The way I responded to a troubled family life was to withdraw and become sullen, closing off not only to everyone else, but to myself as well. I didn't have the slightest idea what I believed in or even what I *felt*. In fact, I thought I never felt a thing.

By the time I got into college, I was very screwed up and basically numb. I had no thoughts or feelings of my own, I was just running on what everyone else had been planning for my life. At the beginning of my third semester, my girlfriend, who was also very unhappy, said, "Bo, this world is such a horrible place, I'm going to kill myself. I'm serious. I'm going to do it on Saturday night. Will you do it with me?" And, numb as I was, my reply was, "Sure — I'm not busy Saturday night."

The day came, and we got nineteen bottles of sleeping pills and divided them by our body weight. I took twelve bottles and she took seven. We wrote suicide notes — pretty much the standard, "It's no one's fault, we just don't fit in here... ." We laid down on a bed at a motel out on Ponchartrain Highway in New Orleans, and we both passed out.

Everything went black. The next thing I knew, I was sitting a couple of feet away from some guy, talking to him. I didn't know who he was or what we were talking about. All I knew was how much I didn't like him.

The dislike got stronger and stronger as he droned on about something or other, and it turned into the most intense hatred and loathing I had ever experienced. I hated the way he looked, the way he talked, the way he held himself, his attitude, his expression, the way he dressed — there wasn't a single thing about this guy that I didn't *detest*. I hated anybody who could possibly like him! I hated his ancestors! I hated everything he might have stood for! Everything about him disgusted me.

Suddenly, there was a loud sound to my left, and the motel room door came crashing open with a bunch of cops rushing in saying, "There he is, get the stomach pump, get the stomach pump!" As it turned out, I had been sitting on the edge of the motel bed, and as I turned my head towards all the commotion, my eyes caught sight of the edge of the big mirror that I had been looking into. All in an instant my mind was reeling. *Oh my god, that's me I hate so much! That obnoxious, arrogant, despicable guy is me!!*

So there I was, having the deepest, most painful revelation of my life, and all these cops and paramedics were trying to hold me down and shove a tube down my throat. I'm like, "Hey, guys, I'm having a *moment* here, can't you see that?" (It's really very funny several decades afterward.)

I spent the night in a jail cell, screaming and hallucinating the scariest things imaginable. That's how they handled 18-year-old suicidal kids in those days — throw 'em in jail. It took me many years to heal from that experience and put all that pain to good use. But it's a powerful lesson of how far off we can go when we lose contact with the simple voice of our own hearts. (My girlfriend survived too, by the way, and is still a friend — and a grandmother now.)

Recognition Versus Choice

One of the deepest lessons I learned is that our beliefs and values are not simply a matter of conscious choice. I thought I had chosen not to have any values; maybe you think so too, because of all the pain you've experienced or the times you've been betrayed and let down. But we all do have very strong values in our hearts. We can't begin leading a happy, productive life until we recognize what they are and begin to live according to them.

Very often, our *deepest* values and beliefs are exactly opposite of our ego's *choices* of values and beliefs. For example, most of us do deeply believe that stealing is wrong. But look at how many excuses we give ourselves for stealing — *it's no big thing; they deserve it; it's a big corporation; I need it more than she does; he'd do it to me if he had the chance,* etc.

It is the same thing with living simply. In our deepest hearts, most of us truly believe that a simple, uncluttered life is healthier for ourselves, our families, and the planet. The ego may shout, *But you need this, and should have that, and protect yourself from that....*

Well, the ego can shout anything it wants, but if we don't find a way to recognize and live by our true values, we're going to screw up our lives royally. Many of us have already.

We can try to cover the screw-ups with rationalizations and all sorts of excuses, or an "I don't give a shit, anyway" attitude, but we can never fool our own hearts — and frankly, no one else cares about our excuses or philosophies. How other people experience us has a lot more to do with our essence than our words. **And if we secretly hate ourselves, our essence isn't going to be too impressive, no matter how well our egos perform their endless dances of con**

games and shadow boxing. How we feel inside is eventually going to come out. No way around it.

But there is great news in all this: We are all really good, decent human beings in our hearts. And as tough as it may be sometimes to discover that goodness and live up to it, it's a lot tougher not to. Take it from somebody who tried.

Simple & Good, Good & Simple

In a world which has become far too complex, filled with people who do not recognize their own goodness, don't allow the overwhelming distractions to rob you of your awareness of who you truly are, and the choices you have to make.

You have choices between the classic opposites of selfishness or unselfishness, greed or generosity, faith or fear, love or hate, acceptance or rejection of your life situation. To the degree that we choose the simple and the good, our lives will be a refreshing gift to the world, and will be in harmony with our own deepest nature.

To the degree we choose the other, our lives will be mere statistics of the madness which engulfed human beings at the beginning of the new millenium. This is not just food for thought; it is a vital truth of your life. Set a course for the simple and good, and your struggle will be supported by the greatest powers in creation.

Whatever I Can

This is the true joy of life, the being used up for a purpose recognized by yourself as a mighty one; being a force of nature instead of a feverish, selfish little clod of ailments and grievances, complaining that the world will not devote itself to making you happy.

I am of the opinion that my life belongs to the community, and as long as I live, it is my privilege to do for it whatever I can. I want to be thoroughly used up when I die, for the harder I work, the more I live.

Life is no "brief candle" to me. It is a sort of splendid torch which I have got hold of for a moment, and I want to make it burn as brightly as possible before handing it on to future generations.

— George Bernard Shaw

Communion &
Community

Be still, and know that I Am God.

— Psalm 46:10

Greater love hath no man than this: That a man lay down his life for his fellow man.

— Jesus (John 15:13)

Spiritual practice was never supposed to be complicated, abstract or distant from our daily life. In fact, both religion and philosophy arise from the *most* real, *most* practical questions of our existence, such as:

1. **What am I doing here?**

2. **How can I make my life work?**

Every thoughtful person, not just intellectuals or preachers, wrestles with those basic questions at some time or other.

For thousands of years, religions, philosophies, saints and sages have tried to help us find the answers to those two simple questions. We have usually been content to argue and even kill each other over the *differences* in their teachings, but when we let go of such fearful separateness and look honestly at the *similarities* instead, we discover that the great wisdom traditions all point in exactly the same two directions: Inner transcendence and unselfish behavior.

In response to the first question, "What are we doing here?," the Holy Ones have all told us to look within, look *beyond* the mind, be STILL, go to the Secret Place within the heart.

In other words, they point to an experience of direct contact with the Christ, Allah, Great Spirit, The Almighty, Yahweh, Buddha Mind, etc. A word for this which no tradition would argue with is *Communion*. The great religions and masters tell us to diligently seek Communion. That's what all this talk of personal spiritual practice has been about.

How Can We Make Life Work?

Now, in response to the second question, the holy teachings once again have expressed identical advice, the same ethics and standards for human behavior: Be kind to one another; love thy neighbor as thyself; do unto others as you would have them do unto you; live for a mightier cause than selfishness; serve the poor; make the world a better place.

Another simple, unarguable word sums it up: *Community*. The Holy Ones all tell us to dedicate our lives to the Community.

It's easy to think of family and friends as community, and everyone else as strangers, associates, rivals or even enemies we just have to cope with in order to make a living, do our time, get ahead, etc. It's also easy to think, "I'll practice Communion and Community as soon as I get home from work, as soon as I get out of prison, as soon as my boss stops picking on me, as soon as I get out of debt, as soon as, as soon as...."

But it doesn't work that way. Our community is *exactly* where we are at every moment during the day; *exactly* whom life places in front of us at any time. That's the whole point. That idiot, that lecher, the con, the cop, the snitch, the boss who drives us up the wall, the windbag politician on TV — everyone we see, hear, or meet must be respected as a brother or sister on the path, even if they have no idea there *is* such a thing as a path.

Clearly, this practice of Community is not for cowards; it's challenging and confusing, and it's full-time. The world has become quite a mess from people only practicing it on the Sabbath, or in places where it's easy, or with people who are nice. We need some humble heroes who take it on full time. This means you. Today. *Now.*

Not "as soon as," but now. Not when you get happier, but now. Not when people treat you more fairly, but now. Not when the world is a safer, kinder place. *NOW.* In the middle of the worst of it.

No one else in the world can play your unique role. God *knows* where you are, *knows* about your depression or anxiety, the people you face, your weaknesses, your past, your fears and doubts. Communion and Community are not for later, they are your tickets out of Hell! If you decide to devote your inner life to Communion and your outer life to Community, that little suffering self doesn't have anywhere to exist!

Don't just say it or plan it; act on it today. The next time you go to work, think about how long you have been there, and then ask yourself honestly whether the office or anyone in it is better off because you have been there. If you are in prison, same thing. Have you made the block a better place to live? Get going. Make Communion and Community real.

If you help even one person or creature to feel safer or more loved, you will be on the road to the Great Recovery.

The Great Recovery

Sita and I have visited a lot of drug recovery programs, both inside and outside of prisons. We've spoken to many people who have been through the doors not just once, but two, three, four, five times — good people with decent hearts and a lot of sincerity, but who keep finding themselves caught in addiction.

They ask, "Why? Why can't I lead a good life? Why do I keep screwing everything up?" I asked many of them what their treatment goals were, and received the same answer I've heard for over twenty years: "I just want to stay clean and sober, get a decent job, get back with my family, have a nice little place to live, a decent set of wheels... I'm a good person; I deserve it, don't I?"

Those goals sound right, don't they? They would be celebrated on talk shows and in self-help books. But are they enough to create a happy life? "Me and mine" is basically what they amount to. "Me and my family." "Me and my buddies." The practice of Community gets reduced to just a few people you love the most. Is that all we were born to care about?

The Great Recovery is from the terrible addiction of self-centered living. That's the recovery all the prophets and sages have encouraged us to seek. Our whole modern world is hooked on looking out for number one, yet the more we do it, the worse we feel. So we increase the dosage. It's the classic pattern of addiction.

It is fascinating to investigate the anatomy of substance abuse recovery failures. You generally find two types — one which occurs during the first year, and the other between the second and third years.

The people who fall off the wagon during the first year seem to crumble because they fail to achieve one or more of those standard goals: Their spouse kicks them out, or they can't find a decent job, etc., and they give up pretty quickly. It's an easy situation to understand: They didn't reach their goals, so they got discouraged and gave up.

But here's the fascinating part: The people who crumble between the second and third years seem to fail *because* they reach their goals. Everyone has been there for them, gone out on a limb for them, they have been loved and fed and employed... .

Then that old constant craving begins again, and they keep it as a deep secret, until they are filled with shame and guilt, thinking "I must be a really horrible, ungrateful person to be craving drugs again after everyone has helped me so much. I must be rotten to the core." From there it's a pretty quick slide to, "I may as well go ahead and get it over with; I'll never be any good, so they may as well find out already."

The real tragedy is that they're not bad people, they simply didn't understand that their "me and mine" goals were simply not big enough goals. They got what they wanted, and something inside was still empty and craving, because "me and mine" is not enough to make a whole, happy human being. Not wickedness, but simple ignorance, was responsible for their failure. Has it happened to you, too? Will it happen next time?

Soul Power

Few of us are ever in the ideal situation where everyone around us changes at the same time, or all the rules suddenly become fair. Most of the time we have to start this humble hero's journey by ourselves, with little or no support. But then we receive the *invisible* support of Truth itself, because Community and Communion are truer ways than fear and selfishness. As Malcolm X discovered in prison, there is *soul-power* in taking a True Path. The harder it is, the more soul-power we gain. **If it weren't so hard, we wouldn't gain so much commitment, courage, and faith.** If it weren't so hard, Jesus, Mohammed, Moses, Buddha and the rest would have preached to us from comfortable thrones instead of showing us their teachings through persecution, discomfort, and rejection. It's hard because that's what it takes to move us beyond the ego; once we do, life isn't so hard anymore; even with all the same conditions in place, we find true peace and dignity.

Breathing Out, Breathing Out, Breathing Out...

So this "Whatever I Can" portion of the book is about community — that part of the Spiritual Journey which requires us to look beyond our own personal needs and attachments. We all have a deep desire to help out; to do some good in the short time we've got left on Earth. We may or may not be aware of that desire; years of self-centered living may have covered it over in some of us. But it's there, I promise.

However, we must remember Communion as well as Community. Trying to dedicate yourself entirely through outward activity, no matter how much you seem to be helping others, will sooner or later chew you up and spit you out if you don't take time for inner silence. It's like trying to breathe out all the time without breathing in. How long can that last? Be sure you breathe in, too, so that you're helping others from a deeper place.

If you know — really know — that all religions boil down to Communion and Community, you could meet the Pope or the Dalai Lama, an imam or minister, rabbi or medicine man, and they would welcome you as a holy friend and agree that you understand the heart of their religions: An **inner** journey beyond all words, and an **outward** path of devoting ourselves to others. Countless different *methods* may exist, but they all lead in those same two directions.

...The Other Tastes Salt

Let there be such oneness between us that when one cries, the other tastes salt.

-- Rosabelle Belleve

The goal of our life should not be to find joy in marriage, but to bring more love and truth into the world. We marry to assist each other in this task.

— Leo Tolstoy

The passages above address the two important prongs of any discussion about marriage. First, Belleve points to the awesome depth of intimacy possible between two people — "when one cries, the other tastes salt." Imagine that.

To balance that intimacy, Tolstoy reminds us that marital self-centeredness is no loftier than individual self-centeredness. As individuals or as a couple, he exhorts us to remember that our purpose is to "bring more love and truth into the world," not just to have an enjoyable life with one other person.

It may sound as though those two views are in conflict with each other. But Tolstoy would have no problem with Belleve's statement, so long as both husband and wife don't stop there. They can use such profound oneness as a springboard into the *big* Profound Oneness. In other words, they would be heading for the day when they could say, "When *anyone* cries, we *both* taste salt." That's the love of the sages and saints. And that's the potential of marriage as a path of service.

The Heart Of God

Practicing marriage as a path of service is to understand that as we open our hearts in love for our spouse or children, we are given the opportunity to keep opening, all the way into the heart of God. We can be more generous to the panhandler because we're in love; be quicker to forgive the person who is annoying or rude or angry, because we're in love; be more in awe of nature, more appreciative of art, music and poetry, because we're in love. We can allow intimate love to awaken us to all of life rather than fixate us toward one person.

> I like your smile and your fingertips,
> I like the way that you move your lips,
> I like the cool way you look at me.
> Everything about you is bringing me misery.
>
> —Bob Dylan

Self-centered love is contractive and possessive, while spiritual love is expansive and generous. Romance and marriage can lead either way, so it is extremely important for you to consider these things *before* you "fall in love," and certainly before you get married. If one of you wants the small love and one the Big Love, you'd be off your rocker to marry each other. You need to marry someone who also wishes to use marriage as a spiritual path. Even then, it is not an easy path. I don't know of an easy path into the heart of God.

love or LOVE

Of course, the popular sentiment in our day is toward small love, not Big Love. To practice marriage as a spiritual path, and especially as a path of service, requires a lot of courage and insight to see through many layers of brainwashing we are exposed to in all the media.

Small love is what sells records and perfumes and Valentine's Day gifts and movies and soap operas. Magazines pitch breakthroughs like "how to keep your sexual life passionate and exciting after ten years of marriage" and other such articles, mostly sharing degrading ideas such as meeting your husband at the door wearing nothing but saran wrap and other such nonsense.

There's nothing wrong with a husband and wife trying to keep their sexual passion alive. Judaism advises us that enjoying each other sexually is one of the duties of a marriage and a gift from God. It may help to keep us happy and balanced, so that we are better members of our community. Where we fall off the path is seeing it as the whole thing or even the most important part. It's just a part, nothing more. And it fades in time, no matter how much saran wrap you buy.

Not only does time diminish or extinguish sexual passion, but so does circumstance. Look at the actor Christopher Reeve, who played *Superman* in several movies in the 1980's. One moment he's muscular, healthy and gorgeous, and the next moment he suffers a fall while riding his horse, and breaks his neck, never to walk again.

His beautiful wife goes from being his passionate romantic partner to being his primary caregiver who must help remove the feces from his bowels. If romance and sexual excitement were very important parts of their marriage, then a tragedy like this would appear to end their relationship. But their path together has just begun.

Their marriage becomes a path of service for her to a degree she never could have imagined. And because of her love and support, he too is able to forge a path of service promoting spinal-injury research. This couple has allowed their compassion and commitment to each other to spill over into compassion and commitment to others. That's the way marriage can work.

This is not to say it was a wonderful thing that happened, or that he and his wife are happy as larks. No couple hopes for something like that. They must have been terrified of the challenges when it first happened. Maybe they're still terrified. But the marriage vows cover it, don't they? *In Sickness or in health, so long as you both shall live.* The vows are not vague or ambiguous. **If your prospective marriage partner is not someone whom you would care for after a tragedy or illness, then don't get married.** Please.

What It's Like to be Loved By God

As we fall in love with another person romantically, for one reason or another, they look at us and see the very best. Other people may look at us and say, "What's the big deal?" But our beloved looks at us and says to them, "Can't you see? (S)he's so beautiful, so genuine, so deep, so wonderful!"

What we see in each other is true, but of course it is not the full story. If we move in with each other, if we get married, if we stay together enough years, we will also see the lowest and worst parts of each other; the selfish side, the fearful side, the petty and weak, the dysfunctional and even perverted sides. If we really open up to each other, we cannot see only what is pretty. We will shame ourselves, we will hurt our beloved in ways we can never take back.

If our mate continues to love us after all that, then something begins to dawn in us: God sees everything too, and if our spouse, a mere human being, can still love us through all our crap, then maybe God loves us as well. Accepting this love for the totality of who we are could be the most profound realization of our life.

What It's Like to Love as God Loves

While we can use the experience of our partner's love to help us feel what it is like to be loved by God, it is almost impossible to love as God loves until we have a child. Our mate has the power to hurt us because s/he knows all the buttons to push. Until we are very, very old and wise, there's always going to be some effort required in loving our spouse through the rough times.

But our love for a baby is as effortless as God's love for us. We look down into that crib and see an angel who needs us and trusts us and depends on us for everything. We see the clear eyes of a soul who sees no wrong in us to forgive, no weakness to overlook, no buttons to push, no power over us except the power of pure love. The contact is soul to soul, no grudges or obstacles in the way. Without hesitation, we would take a bullet for that baby, or step in front of a train. Or even ascend the cross, as Jesus did from his love for us.

Our love for an infant may be as close as a human being can come to loving as God loves. As that baby grows up and develops a selfish side, a petty side, a nasty side and so forth, we don't see a selfish, petty or nasty *person*, we see our beautiful baby who means well but is caught up in selfishness, pettiness and nastiness. Even if our baby lands on death row, we say, "He really isn't a bad person, you know, he's really good underneath all his problems." And we are absolutely right. That's how God sees us. And this is the training we can use for learning to love others as God loves. That's how the saints love us all.

> The lowest of the low you can think of, is dearer to me than your only son is to you.
>
> — The Baal Shem Tov

The Service of Letting Go

If marriage helps us to love as God loves, we must also bear in mind that "God so loved the world, he gave his only begotten son..." That is to say, marriage also gives us the profound mystery of bearing the excruciating grief of losing each other; bearing this pain in a way which does not act surprised or outraged or bitter over the natural rhythms of life and death. This is a much-needed aspect of service in a culture which worships youth and runs from pain.

> Love, to be real, it must cost — it must hurt — it must empty us of self.
>
> — Mother Teresa

For example, look at me and Sita. People have said they envy our marriage and that now, after thirty-three years, it must be so easy for us. Many of the ego dramas do fade away, but when Sita looks into my face now she sees a gray-haired, grandfatherly man instead of the young stud she married. My hearing isn't what it used to be. My vision isn't what it used to be. It's no joke; after weathering countless storms with each other, one of us is going to lose the other to time.

101

I was nineteen when we got married. We have been married virtually our whole lives. Yet when one of us dies, it will seem much too soon no matter when it happens. We've worked together, raised a child together, seen the world together, shared one taste in music, humor, movies, books and scriptures, nursed each other through serious illnesses. We can't conceive of a world without the other in it. The names Bo and Sita are spoken together so much that people have written it as one person: "Boensita Lozoff." Can you imagine the grief of the survivor?

If this softens your heart a little, then our marriage continues to be a path of service even now, as we consider the grief it will bring when one of us is widowed. The fundamental reality of a life of service is always an openhearted connection to others, not just in joy, but in sorrow as well. Our joys and sorrows unite us with the joys and sorrows of all people. To close off and label them "private" is to miss their purpose. Our life itself is our friendship with the world.

This is what it means for marriage to be a path of service. Two people become one couple. They wear rings on one particular finger so that anyone can recognize at a glance that they're not just individuals anymore. It's no less of a symbol than monks wearing robes. Both rings and robes serve to identify those people who have chosen a full-time, committed spiritual path.

This is the potential Marriage holds. Don't settle for less. You *can* know what it means to truly taste the salt of your beloved's tears. And then you can begin to understand what it means to taste the salt of the world's tears. From that place comes true compassion, and a deep desire to be of service to the world. These are qualities that saints from every tradition have told us are the keys to the Kingdom of Heaven.

To Be Able

"What is the best of all things that are praised?"

"Skill."

The Mahabharata

I once got a phone call from a young man in Atlantic City, New Jersey. He said, "A friend of mine told me I was heading down the wrong road, and that I really need to get your books to steer me back in the right direction." I asked him what wrong road he was taking, and he said he was using drugs again. He has been out of prison for a few years and has been doing "so-so," but he knew that he was starting the Big Slide again and was desperate for help.

I said, "Well, you don't need my books to know that drugs are going to screw up your life. You need to do whatever it takes — twelve steps, counseling, detox, whatever — to stop using drugs immediately. You have to stop. You already know that. Don't wait for my books. You need to do it today."

He said he had already been through groups and rehab, and maybe he would go again, but wasn't sure how long it would hold up. So I asked him to tell me what his life was about. He said that he had an apartment and worked at Bally's Casino. That's it. That's his life.

I told him I'd probably be doing drugs too if that were all my life was about — working every day in a greed-filled, decadent environment; witnessing pathetic gamblers, prostitutes, drug dealers, gangsters, wealthy people, poor people, young people, and elderly people, wasting their time in pursuits that have absolutely *nothing* to do with the meaning or purpose of human life.

I told him that if all he's doing is working there and going back and forth to his apartment — that's not life, that's hell. He was silent for a while.

I asked him what he believed in. What is important to him? What brings him joy? What noble cause, what passion, inspires him? He remained silent for another minute and then said, "I don't know; just living. You know, just hanging out."

I asked him what he was good at or interested in — anything that he might strive to become better at, like carpentry, auto mechanics, music, art or anything at all. "I don't know. Nothing, I guess."

I told him we'd send our books, but there was no magic recipe which will help him create a delicious life out of such rancid ingredients. He needs a bigger change.

I encouraged him to look into his heart, talk with others, develop some worthwhile interests, and find a cause he can believe in and work hard to support.... Finally he meekly said, "Well, listen, um, thanks for sending me the books; I appreciate you taking the call," and hung up the phone.

Becoming a Mensch

How is it that millions of people in our modern society reach adulthood having almost no values, interests or useful skills? It is a big mistake to assume that this is just a matter of underprivileged kids needing a better education. Privileged kids are just as lost, apathetic, and sometimes even *less* skilled in practical things like fixing a flat tire or repairing a leaky roof.

These days, few kids of *any* socio-economic group feel any link to their ancestors' honor or their unborn children's' future, or any ideal larger than "I don't know, just living. You know, just hanging out."

In her book, *Jesus Meets Buddha*, Sister Ayya Khema says that in the Buddha's Lovingkindness Discourse, one of his most famous, he lists fifteen qualities which are essential for a good life. Number one on this list is **"To Be Able."** To be a capable person, to have a variety of skills that come in handy, gives us self-respect, and provides various honorable ways to make a living and be of service.

The Jewish culture has a well-known word for such a person: *Mensch*. A Mensch is someone whom you can loan your car to without worrying about it. It's someone who can figure out how to get the crumbly piece of toast out of the toaster without electrocuting anybody; someone whom you would like to have next to you in a fire, or a stuck elevator, or when the roof leaks.

What does it take to be able, to be a Mensch? It seems to me that it takes three things, which should be the framework of any educational system or model of childraising:

> 1. Learning the classic spiritual and moral **values** which are common to any civilization — mercy, kindness, justice, courage, etc.

2. Learning practical **skills** relevant to the basics — food, shelter, warmth, health. Such self-reliance is the core of self-respect and common sense.

3. Developing **self-discipline** and adaptability so one doesn't fall apart in hard times. Not needing to be pampered. Not being so touchy or needy.

A Different View of Childhood

In the ancient Hindu culture, even the most privileged kids, the children of kings and emperors, were sent into the forest ashrams of rugged sages at a very young age to live without any luxuries and learn true unselfishness.

In most other ancient cultures too, childhood was mainly about learning those three things: **Values, skills, and self-discipline.** This is what gives us a sense of connection to others, a sense of our place in the great scheme of life, a sense of responsibility to the common good. If we separate kids from any duties in the real world, we inadvertently remove their sense of relevance as well.

This is another big reason why modern American kids are so lost and angry. American childhood is unnaturally insulated and separate from the adult world.

"Generation gap" is not a natural human phenomenon; it's a serious problem we've created by having so little to do with our children's daily lives.

Many kids don't know or care what their parents do for a living. The kids themselves make no direct contribution to their family's daily needs or maintenance. Even the government calls children "dependents." Is that a good message?

We may see American childhood as "giving them a chance just to be kids, just to have fun while they can." But in reality, the effect seems to make them bored, helpless and hopeless. People of every age *need* to be useful, and *need* to be skilled at something.

If we provide no opportunities for kids to be responsible, skilled, and needed, no meaningful initiations from one stage of childhood to another, then children will form their own groups. They will form gangs, social cliques, Satanic cults; groups in which they can experience initiation, define their identity and value to the group, pledge their loyalty, and learn the skills relevant to that group — even if the relevant skills happen to be using a credit card to pick a lock, or a complex set of hand signals that cops won't understand.

A Nation of Mensches

Helena Norberg-Hodge, author of *Ancient Futures: Learning from Ladakh,* is a European woman who spent many years living in the tiny Himalayan region of Ladakh. She points out that before our modern Western educational system came to that area, the society was basically a whole *nation* of Mensches!

Children grew up learning their society's values of compassion, nonviolence and harmony, and virtually every boy and girl, by the time they reached adolescence, knew how to grow and prepare food, mend clothes, care for animals, build houses, construct complex irrigation systems. In short, Ladakhi youngsters naturally became moral and capable young adults.

Now "progress" has come. Thousands of children are removed from their villages, crammed into classrooms to memorize facts and recite their times-tables. They no longer learn from their parents, aunts, uncles, grandparents; they no longer share the responsibility of food production, warmth, shelter, childcare; they now have a more "privileged" childhood.

But as Ms. Hodge explains, when their education is finished and they return to their villages, they are essentially useless. They have been cut off from the wealth of values, skills and traditions that have made the Ladakhis a happy people for hundreds of years. Many of them then migrate to the larger cities around India or Nepal, becoming prostitutes or drug abusers or working for minimum wage and being as aimless as the fellow who called me from Atlantic City. It's a very sad situation, similar to the devastation of the Native American cultures in the United States.

Josh's Two Complaints

In 1991, Sita and I celebrated our twenty-fifth wedding anniversary by spending the day with our son Josh in a remote spot at the bottom of the Rio Grande Gorge in northern New Mexico. The three of us took the opportunity to clean out old baggage with each other, air any secrets, deepen our sense of love and connection and loyalty to each other. Josh was twenty at the time.

At one point during the day, I asked Josh if there was any way we had let him down as parents. He said there were actually two ways. "First of all, whenever something was hard for me to do, you guys helped me so much that I didn't develop much self-discipline. That hurt me a lot when I lived in LA. I had to develop all my discipline on my own. You didn't help me become very tough or adaptable.

"The second thing is, Dad, do you remember when I was fourteen and I told you that when I finished high school I wanted to go out to LA to be an actor instead of going to college?" I told him I remembered, and he continued. "Well, you said that I would have your blessing to do so on one condition: That by the time I left home, I was a skilled carpenter. That way, whether I succeeded in my acting career or not, I would still be able to make a good living and feel the satisfaction of working with my hands."

Once again, I told him I remembered. Then Josh said, "But you didn't make me do it. You didn't force me to become a good carpenter, and you gave me your blessing anyway. You should have stuck by your word."

I said, "But I tried! I built five buildings between the time you were fourteen and the time you left home, and I tried to get you to help me on every one of them. It was like pulling teeth to get you to help. So I gave up. I didn't want to force you."

Josh replied, "That's exactly what I mean: You *should* have forced me. You were the parent and I was the kid. You set a condition for your blessing and then you didn't make me live up to it. You should have made me become a good carpenter whether I liked it or not."

He was right. Sita and I asked his forgiveness on both counts. He asked for ours as well. It was a great day — a renewal of deep affection and trust. I recommend such an occasional event to any family. And again, it reminded us that kids don't want to be in a fantasy world of their own. They want to be needed and involved and held accountable, even though they may resist it at the time.

Cutting Out the Old and the Young

In order to feel connected to Life, we must contribute something positive toward the common good. Children and elderly people are no exception. By sheltering children from responsibility and putting the elderly out to pasture, we have unwittingly created an angry, aimless younger generation and a lonely, undervalued older generation.

Many modern Americans assume this is simply what it means to be young or to be old. But anyone who has traveled in other cultures knows this is not true. Children can be happy, respectful, capable. The elderly can be radiantly peaceful, wise, venerated.

Life is a holy and mysterious process all the way through. There are wonders and challenges in every stage of life. Each stage is worthy of equal respect. **Each stage requires values, skill, and self-discipline.** And in every stage, we need each other. We need younger, middle-aged and older people around us, not just others our own age. We are ever and always part of each other. We either walk into Heaven arm in arm or we don't get in at all.

Making the Change

At this moment, there are many millions of angry young people, lonely old people, and lost, unhappy people like our friend in Atlantic City. The situation won't turn around overnight. But each one of us can begin the process of turning it around by sizing up our own lives with respect to values, skills and self-discipline, and doing whatever we need to do in order to bring those qualities up to our liking.

We can look at how we are treating our children and elders and see whether we are allowing them their own areas of usefulness and responsibility.

We can steadily dismantle every notion we have that personal freedom is about money, or accomplishments, prestige, recreation, and we can cease passing such empty notions on to our kids (more on this in the next chapter).

We can develop common sense and basic skills, at any age, so that we become more self-reliant and adaptable to changing circumstances. We can size up our way of talking and make sure that we say what we mean and mean what we say. No hidden agendas or broken promises to ourselves or others.

In short, these are the qualities of a basic *Mensch*, and the world badly needs more Mensches. Values, skills, and self-discipline make for a more enjoyable experience of living, more self-respect and confidence and friendliness to others. We can put ourselves and our kids and our elders back on this time-honored path to freedom and see how it begins to affect the folks next door and down the block. Everyone wants to feel better these days. A humble personal step in the right direction is a contribution to the whole world, a wonderful way to begin a life of service.

A True Education

On June 17th, 1744, the commissioners from Maryland and Virginia negotiated a treaty with the Indians of the Six Nations at Lancaster, Pennsylvania. The Indians were invited to send their boys to William and Mary College. The next day they declined the offer as follows:

We know that you highly esteem the kind of learning taught in those Colleges, and that the Maintenance of our young Men, while with you, would be very expensive to you. We are convinced that you mean to do us Good by your Proposal; and we thank you heartily. But you, who are wise must know that different Nations have different Conceptions of things and you will therefore not take it amiss, if our ideas of this kind of Education happen not to be the same as yours.

We have had some Experience of it. Several of our young People were formerly brought up at the Colleges of the Northern Provinces: they were instructed in all your Sciences; but, when they came back to us, they were bad Runners, ignorant of every means of living in the woods...neither fit for Hunters, Warriors, nor Counselors, they were totally good for nothing.

We are, however, not the less obliged by your kind Offer, tho' we decline accepting it; and, to show our grateful Sense of it, if the Gentlemen of Virginia will send us a Dozen of their Sons, we will take care of their Education, instruct them in all we know, and make Men of them.

— T.C. McLuhan, *Touch the Earth*

The Myth of Personal Freedom

The world would be better off
If people tried to be better.

And people would become better
If they stopped trying to be better off.

For when everybody tries to become better off,
Nobody is better off.

But when everybody tries to become better,
Everybody is better off.

— Peter Maurin, Catholic Worker Movement

Our contemporary notion of Personal Freedom is like a deity at this point in our culture. We have been taught to revere and follow it unquestioningly. But if we want to look at it honestly, this notion doesn't seem to be working out very well, and needs some re-evaluation. The American notion of Personal Freedom goes something like this: Doing whatever we want, when we want, without obligations to others. But that's an infant's view of freedom, not a sage's.

Human beings exist in relation to each other. **Real freedom cannot be separated from responsibility to others.** To be free means to be able to respond to whatever the situation or circumstances may require.

If I don't know how to swim, and I walk by a lake where a child is drowning, I may passionately *want* to save her, but I don't have the freedom to do it. I may have a million dollars in my pocket, I may be President of the United States, but if I haven't learned how to swim, that child will still drown. Even the sincerest motivation is only one part of freedom.

If we are unskilled, self-centered, addicted or greedy, we will not be very free. Merely doing what we want, in a way that ignores our connection with each other or how we best fit together, isn't personal freedom.

In fact, the people who attain such false personal freedom tend to go a bit scooters. When you get rich enough or powerful enough to do whatever you want, like Howard Hughes or Elvis Presley, it isn't much of a life. But for some reason we still cling to that model — "do what I want, when I want, with no obligations or responsibilities. Ah, that's the life!"

How Is It Working?

Everyone would agree that Michael Jordan is one of the most successful athletes of all time. By far the wealthiest and most famous member of his profession, by our cultural definition Michael should have lots of personal freedom to do as he likes.

But a friend of mine traveled extensively with the Chicago Bulls, and so he had a different perspective. He said that everyone else on the team, even other well-known players, were able to take a walk, go out to a restaurant, etc. But Michael couldn't even go to the hotel lobby without it turning into a mob scene. He was basically a prisoner in his hotel room. A *prisoner.*

It's time to start looking at this bill of goods we've been sold about personal freedom. We need to see that many of the attitudes that we consider to be universal beliefs and perspectives are in reality just cultural assumptions.

Many of us have spent time in "third-world" countries, where people don't have the freedom of choice that we have — lots of goals to achieve, lots of dreams to fulfill — because at an early age they begin taking on responsibility for helping their families and communities function. They have obligations that most of us would call limitations on their personal freedom.

It's ironic that people in those cultures often seem to have a higher personal *happiness* quotient than many Americans have. They don't especially feel oppressed. We may think, *boy, they're really prisoners. They have to go into whatever trade their father or mother is in. I wouldn't want to be limited like that. I like having all the options in the world.*

But options to do what? To fool ourselves into thinking we can be everything or do everything? To stay so busy — even in wholesome activities — that we never feel simple peace? We need to be honest and say, "How are we doing as a society with our models of success and personal freedom?"

Well, let's look at a few statistics: Our teen suicide rate has tripled in the last couple of decades, teen homicide has tripled in the last couple of decades, and statistically, our children are the angriest and most violent people in the world. The peak age of violent crime is seventeen now, whereas for a couple of hundred years it stayed at the late twenties. In the last ten years, it's gone down constantly. It is no longer unheard of for an eight-year-old to murder another child.

Tens of millions of Americans, from the homeless to the wealthy, take drugs just to get through the day. Peppermint Prozac is actually now being marketed for children!

So by a lot of objective indicators, our people are not very happy. Yet we're not really questioning our basic models. **What is so hypnotic about this notion of personal freedom, that we're not noticing any objective indicators of how it isn't working?**

A Piece in the Puzzle

Just as we have switched our cultural values around to the point where the notion of "contentment" is regarded negatively, there are many such words that we've devalued in modern times. One is *duty*. Another is *sacrifice*. These values seem to echo from every wisdom tradition and religion, and yet we act as though they are outdated. Duty and sacrifice are now co-dependency.

Those of us who let go of our own personal ambitions in order to fully participate in our families and communities are looked down upon. We are told, "Don't give up your dreams. Your dreams are all that's important." But there's a very important point being missed.

We have to try to re-evaluate these principles in an appropriate way. We must begin to be less arrogant, and turn back to the ancient truths. Giving your life to your community or family doesn't have to be co-dependency; it can be a joyous expression of trust in the process of life itself.

This is a level of trust that many of us have pretty much given up on. And the result is that, for the most part, we now identify our personal agendas as being our lives: What we want to be; what we want to achieve; what we want to do. We don't have faith that there is a life in momentum, in flow.

We have to begin to see that our life was carved out of the same block of God that every other life is carved out of. And that this life is going to have direction and meaning if we ease up on pursuing our own Personal Freedom.

It's a wonderful feeling to let go of something that we really thought we prized and wanted, and wanted to possess. We let go and we say, "Lord, may I be an instrument of your peace," and we just die into it.

We think to ourselves, *boy I thought I was going to be pursuing that degree, but working with these kids really seems to be important, and so I'll keep doing that instead.*

As we do, we begin to feel levels of relief that are unbelievable, and we say "Ah the joy! Ah, the joy not to be so personally involved in my life anymore, but to be involved with these ageless principles of living simply, doing spiritual practice, and trying to be of service."

So we may very well go back to school, or carve out a career. **We may still end up with that degree, but it's because we believe that it's the best way we can contribute.** We do it because the world needs doctors and plumbers, teachers and truck drivers.

Then the puzzle starts fitting better with all the people around us, and the problems in our community, and in the world. Maybe we wind up doing a different part of it than we thought we'd do, but it's a team effort, and we have obligations and responsibilities — to our family, our community, our country, our world; to the Spiritual Journey.

Obligations and responsibilities are an important component of a good life; they are not merely burdens. Even though they may sometimes be demanding, our duties help us to feel *a part of* the people around us rather than *apart from* them.

An Easy Trap

Watching the portrayal of modern life on television or in movies, it is easy to understand how we develop a warped desire for a notion of personal freedom which separates and elevates us above others and supposedly frees us from responsibilities so we can enjoy endless pleasure. But this is merely a myth, and we are adults; we don't have to swallow it hook, line and sinker.

No great sages have ever encouraged us to think of ourselves first, first, first, always ourselves first, like the popular media culture does. With good intentions, Oprah Winfrey may coach her audiences, "Learn how to say I WANT," but you won't find that teaching in any of the Wisdom Traditions. The great teachings all tell us to take reasonable care of our basic needs, and then move beyond that sense of "me" into the heart of what life is really about — helping others.

"But Enough About Me..."

"Why are you unhappy? Because 99% of the things you do, think, and feel are about yourself. And there isn't one!"

— Wei Wu Wei

S ome years ago I gave a talk at Duke University, and as I walked across the campus, my eye was pulled toward a sign that was posted on nearly every telephone pole and bulletin board. It looked something like this:

FEEL GOOD
ABOUT YOURSELF

Give Blood.
See the American Red Cross today.

Now, that's the final straw! Enough already. This is getting embarrassing. The current self-esteem fad is going to be something our grandchildren laugh about like we laugh about disco music, pet rocks and hula-hoops. The purpose of doing a good deed is *not* to feel good about yourself. That may be a *by-product*, but if we make it the goal instead, we miss the whole point.

True **self-esteem is like a smile: It arises naturally in a life lived well.** We don't stand in front of the mirror all day *working* on our smile, do we? We don't wake up in the morning thinking "Now, let's see; I've got to smile today; I've got to smile; I've got to smile..." Countless things effortlessly bring a smile to our faces — nice people, a beautiful sky, a little baby, our old jalopy starting right up instead of having to drag out the jumper cables. Smiling is a natural part of life.

So are self-esteem and personal happiness. They are impossible goals if pursued selfishly, yet they are free gifts when we give up self-absorption. **Mother Teresa didn't undertake her mission in order to boost her self-esteem.** She followed her heart; she did what she felt was *right*. Without focusing on self-centered happiness, she dedicated her life to helping others. The result? A profoundly happy person, naturally esteemed by the world.

Ripping Off the Poor

Back to the Red Cross signs — you may say, "Hey, what's wrong with appealing to a little self-interest in order to get people to do the right thing?" Plenty. The Red Cross is one of the most respected humanitarian organizations in the world. Those signs imply to a whole generation of young adults that everybody should just be out for themselves.

What used to be a charitable act becomes merely one more strategy for selfish happiness. Instead of *giving* to the needy, we're just ripping them off to get a little buzz. They may get the blood, but they used to get a whole heap of kindness with it, which may be lacking until we and the Red Cross come to our senses.

It's one thing to hear someone say, "I feel so good when I'm volunteering at the soup kitchen." But it's quite another to build advertising campaigns around it as the *main* reason to volunteer. Altruism — the act of doing something for the benefit of others — must *actually* be altruistic. "Will it benefit me?" I don't know! That's not what we should be thinking about.

Of course, we all know in the back of our minds that altruistic people are often the happiest, most dynamic people in the world. We've all heard that caring for the needs of others is important to our own well-being. I'm not saying we should pretend not to know that human service is a time-honored path associated with deep peace and happiness. **But we need to remember that it's not a path *about* our happiness; rather, it's a happy *path*.**

When we begin to care more about others than ourselves — what early Christians called "Self-forgetfulness" and what Buddhists call "Bodhicitta" — the happiness we feel is mainly a sense of *relief* more than anything else.

It's a happy relief to step aside from the spotlight of ego's endless desires and fears. It's a happy relief to open ourselves to what we are really and truly about: Love, compassion, courage, kindness, mercy, dedication. Happiness is our natural state when we live a spirit-centered, service-centered lifestyle.

The Self-Esteem Trap

Self-esteem seems to have become nothing short of a new American religion. The problem is, low self-esteem and high self-esteem are *both* egomania. If a river is in flood, raging toward your house, do you care whether the water is hot or cold? It's the **volume** of water which is the problem, not the temperature! Cold or hot, you drown!

The same is true of self-centeredness. If I think I'm the greatest thing ever to hit the Earth, that's just as much of an ego problem as if I'm wrapped up in myself with worthlessness, guilt, doubt, etc. **The solution to a negative ego problem is not to replace it with a positive ego problem.**

We seem to worship individuality as though we each exist in our own separate universe — which of course is untrue. And because it is untrue, what may once have been individuality has now mutated into alienation. Community esteem has been sacrificed to self-esteem.

Classic Vices Are Now Called Virtues

In the same way that modern-day America has given negative connotations to classic virtues such as duty and contentment, we're also probably the first society since the fall of Rome to make personal pride a prized virtue instead of a dangerous vice. Pride is in, modesty is out. Assertiveness is in, easygoingness is out. Boastfulness is in, humility is out. Competitiveness is in, self-sacrifice is out. These are not good signs.

We tell our children, "Oh don't be modest. You've got to shout, you've got to celebrate your gifts, child! The only way to get ahead is to blow your own horn." We're raising assertive, aggressive, pushy kids, and they're not happy. They're pretty angry.

We mean well, but we're not thinking clearly. **We hear one "expert" say that we should praise our kids, and the next day somebody begins cranking out millions of bumper stickers saying "My child is an honor student at Smith Junior High."** That's not praise, it's tacky boastfulness. And it doesn't take the place of spending more *time* with our kids.

Frankly, kids need to be *appreciated* a lot more than they need to be praised. Appreciation takes more time and commitment. It's a lot more work than merely uttering some popular slogans or slapping one more bumper sticker on our car.

Appreciation joins and unites, while praise tends to separate and elevate. When we say, "Oh, sweetheart, I am so glad to be spending this time with you, and I treasure you so much in my life," that's appreciation. And it means a tremendous amount to our children without making them feel superior to the kid next door.

But when we merely throw praise around, or slap the bumper sticker on the car, it's no longer the whole child we are valuing, but rather one or two things that the child is doing — and usually doing *better* than other children. That sort of praise is a strengthening of ego instead of a strengthening of humanity.

The Great News

But there is good news in all of this — in fact, it's *great* news. There's a wonderful reason that personal pride, high self-esteem, boastfulness, and selfish success don't lead to real happiness. I've said it many times already: **We are all deeply connected.** We are in this thing together from start to finish. We are One Big Family, like it or not. I've come to like it. I hope you do too. We *need* each other.

If we were able to find true happiness through selfish pursuits, *that* would be the tragedy, because it would mean our essential nature is not deep or compassionate. **Our society is terribly unhappy precisely because our true nature is divine and generous and merciful, and we're not acting like it.** That really is great news.

It means we can save ourselves. We *can* wake up from this horrible national hangover. Enough of the arrogance and pride and "I'm special!" affirmations. It's all really just silly attempts to cover our fear, confusion, and insecurity. Enough of lavishing empty praise on our kids and friends and ourselves. Enough of the "I deserve abundance" seminars and "Free yourself from guilt" workshops. Enough about "me" already!

We need to look around and realize that we only exist in relation to each other. And then we need to act like it.

We Need You!

If not you, who? If not now, when?

— Hillel

B efore the modern age, before jet travel and worldwide news reports, before telephones and the internet, most human beings lived their whole lives in one community and didn't have a great deal of continual information about what was happening anywhere else.

To dedicate yourself to service was a pretty straightforward endeavor, and you could see the difference you made pretty clearly. If you fed the hungry, you would see them gain weight day by day; if you taught skills to the unemployed, you would see them gain employment and get on with their lives.

In today's world, the faces of the poor shift and change every day. There seem to be an endless number of homeless, unemployed, unskilled, abandoned, addicted, luckless human beings whose problems far exceed whatever fleeting help we may be able to offer them. We turn on the evening news and are reminded of countless other problems across the globe which seem once again to be far beyond our ability to change.

It is easy for us to feel so overwhelmed that we feel our acts of service are essentially meaningless, and therefore, unnecessary. "What good can I do?" "What difference would it make?" "It would just be to make myself feel better!" "The problems are beyond repair." "I'll give an annual donation to United Way."

Even when we contact charitable agencies to inquire about volunteering, their response (or lack of one) may deepen our feeling that we are not needed. Many nonprofit organizations are terrible about returning phone calls or responding to requests for information. Some may make you feel they are only interested in your wallet and not your help — and, sadly, sometimes that's true!

But I swear to you, it is not true that you are unneeded. It is not true that your compassionate service is a waste of time or a mere feel-good tactic for yourself. Compassionate service is very profound. It is a relationship not just to the person or people you are serving, but a relationship to life itself; a whole way of being in the world — even if you presently live in prison.

> If, after trying to save the world, the world is lost...
> No regrets.
>
> — His Holiness The Dalai Lama

It is true that your acts of kindness may not solve the problems of hunger, poverty, racism, pollution, prison life, etc. But the goal is not a problem-free world. The goal is attainable right here and now — a state of love, goodwill and helpfulness between you and at least some of the people around you, instead of fear, distrust and selfishness.

This is the same teaching Jesus tried to get across about the Kingdom of Heaven: It's not out there or up ahead; it's *at hand*. Right here, between you and the person next to you. Or else, we never get there.

Tikkun

The Kingdom of Heaven is a way of life, a path of kindness and service and unselfishness. Such a lifestyle enables us to feel our true nature now, even while the larger problems exist.

We may not know how to bring about a world which is free from hunger, but we do know that by feeding a few people, we bring more kindness into the world right now. We have the means, no matter what anyone else does or doesn't do. The sages tell us that our actions, however humble, make a difference in the whole world, not just the spot where we are standing.

Tikkun is a Hebrew word which means "world repair." When I first heard this word, it struck me that it refers more to a basic instinct than to any type of activity. We may pray to be blessed with *tikkun*; in other words, to see the whole world with an eye toward helping out. It describes a view, a state of mind and heart, which becomes our basic nature, our effortless attitude.

This spirit of *tikkun* is the essence of compassionate service — not *how much* good we do, but rather waking and sleeping, eating and breathing, working and playing, with an ever-present attitude of kindness to people, animals, and everything else in our immediate vicinity at any given time; no time off.

Take A Step

But talk is cheap. At some point we have to take a step, and there are countless good steps to take. Tying in several of the themes in this book, for example, you could stop spending time and money on television, video games, and movies, and make a family decision of how to spend the same amount of time in service to your community instead.

Most communities have many volunteer opportunities which may be coordinated through a local library, a volunteer coordinating agency, or an interfaith council of local churches. Start finding out what's going on in your community and see what draws your interest. Don't wait until you're "ready;" take a step now.

If you want to leap rather than step, decide to spend some family vacation time on what is now called a "volunteer vacation," whereby you and your family would travel somewhere to participate in a special charitable project.

The University of Chicago Press publishes a book by Bill McMillon called *Volunteer Vacations*, listing hundreds of organizations that need short-term volunteers. Another source of information is Volunteers for Peace, at 43 Tiffany Road in Belmont, Vermont. They publish an annual directory of hundreds of "work camps" all over the globe.

Most cities in America, and a growing number around the world, have local chapters of Habitat for Humanity, a wonderful organization that builds homes for the poor. Habitat relies almost entirely on volunteer labor. Depending on the ages of your children, it could be a wonderful family involvement in your own community.

Or it could be an unforgettable far-flung experience. One friend of mine is so inspired by his local Habitat experiences that he's now considering joining one of Habitat's international projects, where he, his wife and three young kids would live and work at a Habitat site in Africa for three years. What an extraordinary opportunity for those kids! **Imagine the skills they'll learn, the values they'll develop, their cultural breadth and wealth of experience by the time they return home.** Now that's education!

"But What Can I Do?"

But don't wait until you get to Africa or India to begin being of service. Start where you are. Pitch in to help make your community a better place, even if your community is a prison.

I often hear about wonderful service projects happening behind bars, from formal programs, like reading books onto tape for the blind or making quilts for AIDS babies, to inmates who are just trying to make their cellblock a kinder place to live.

Our friend Tom Dodson is doing time at the Ellis Unit in Huntsville, Texas. Disheartened by the thefts in his cellblock, Tall Tom (as he's known) posted the following sign:

ATTENTION: THERE IS A CELL THIEF ON THIS TANK!!!

> I find the behavior of stealing from other men on D-12 to be unacceptable. I publicly proclaim my dissatisfaction with this behavior.

> I hereby commit myself to working toward a non-violent solution to this situation.

> I encourage anyone who has similar feelings to join in a moment of silence at 5:45 am. You are encouraged to approach this period of silent contemplation with a feeling of peacefulness and community unity toward all men on D-12. Your support in this effort is appreciated.

Underneath, Tall Tom left a place for signatures, and nine other men signed on. He says that from the time he posted the sign, there's been no stealing reported in his tank. He'll never know how many men participated in the silent meditation, but the sign obviously had an effect on lots of the guys.

This is a solid beginning of community organizing. There is *always* an opportunity to be of service. And prisons especially need your kindness and helpfulness, don't they? You may not want to be there, but millions of people in the "free world" also live in dangerous, ugly places where they would rather not be. That doesn't mean you can avoid doing your part.

Don't Just Keep Your Head Down

And if you're getting released from prison soon, *please* don't get out here looking for what you can get, but rather come out and see what you can give. People out here have been working their butts off while you've been inside. Come home with the attitude of, "Sorry I haven't been here to do my part; how can I help?" That's the healthiest and most truthful way to come back to the free world without heading back to the joint in three or four months.

You may be hearing advice from family or fellow inmates that goes something like; "get a little job, a little apartment, keep your head down, and just stay out of trouble."

Even with the most sincere and forgiving element of society, it seems as though the general attitude toward ex-cons is something like, "If you convince us you're rehabilitated, and you stay clean and sober, we'll *let* you back into society." Don't buy into that view of what your life on the outside should be about.

Here's the truth: WE NEED YOU. Really. We're not doing so hot out here. Our kids are angry and confused, we're knocking ourselves out trying to achieve some level of "success" that doesn't even exist, and we've generally abandoned our true faith in the Transcendent, in the Glory of God.

We Need You! We need your experience. We need your wisdom. This culture needs to see people who have had all their "stuff" taken away from them, and have discovered that they didn't need so much stuff in the first place. What a great example you can be for your kids who think that getting the latest video game will make them happy.

Plug into the problems in your community; share your experiences and ideas. There's usually at least one local group, minister or community organizer who is trying to improve the neighborhood. Find them and join up. If you're religious, find a church of your denomination and speak to the pastor honestly about who you are and where you've been. Offer yourself in any way you can be of help.

The kids in your neighborhood especially need to meet some truly good people who are not lily-white goody-goody, but are **real**, like you. Neither lie about your past, nor carry on about it. Let them meet a real adult who has been humbled by his or her pain, and is transforming it into compassion, peace, and simple happiness. Give your life away to your community and see what you get back.

We all have a helpful part to play, wherever we live. The notion of "doing my own time" does not lead to a successful spiritual life. We need you to do your part. Are you ready and willing? The world is anxiously awaiting your help.

> There are many people who can do big things. But there
> are very few people who will do the small things.
> — Mother Teresa

12 Practices for a Deep & Simple Life

Therefore I shall put this way of life into actual practice.

For what can be achieved by merely talking about it?

Will a sick man be benefited merely by reading the medical texts?

—Shantideva

The Power of Practice

On the first day of school, a teacher tells the class they are going to study numbers, and they will do it by taking one number each day and discussing it. That day, she teaches them about the number "one." On the second day of class, the teacher asks, "Is everyone ready to move on to number "two?" All the students except one young boy raise their hands. The teacher notices the boy, and says, "Well, since everyone else is ready, you'll just have to continue studying the number "one" at home.

Several days go by. Each day the class progresses to the next number, and each day the same boy is the only one who isn't ready to move on. In fact, he tells the teacher he is still studying the number "one." She finally becomes so frustrated that she sends him home and says, "When you are ready to move on to the next number, you can come back to school."

Several weeks go by, and the young boy finally comes back to class. With a sneer, the teacher says, "Oh, are you finally ready to move on now?" The boy nods his head obediently. Continuing to mock him, the teacher says, "Well, why don't you come up to the blackboard and show the class all you've learned about the number "one?"

The boy gets up from his seat, walks to the blackboard, picks up the chalk, and stands quietly for a moment. Then he draws a simple "**1**" on the blackboard, whereupon the blackboard shatters and falls in pieces from the power of the boy's touch.

-- A Sufi story

134

Introduction

Now is the time to get to work. Remember the caution by Trungpa Rinpoche near the beginning of this book: "*Reading spiritual books is like reading the menu at a restaurant. Don't forget, you must eat the meal.*"

Taoist master Lao Tzu says, "*With all this talking, what has been said? The subtle truth can be pointed at with words, but it can't be contained by them.*" Each tradition has its own way of issuing the same warning. Basically, we can't just learn it. We have to *do* it. We have to turn The Word into flesh.

Because spiritual practices work deeply and naturally, they usually require commitment and patience. **I recommend that if you wish to explore a spiritual practice, take a vow to perform that practice for at least one month, at the same time every day, before evaluating whether you like it or not or whether it's "working" in any way.** The "Vow Practice" chapter in this section gives tips for how to go about that.

It is also important to have a correct view about spiritual practice right from the beginning. The point of these practices is not to "escape the pressures" or "get your mind off your problems" or anything along those lines. Quite the contrary — the purpose of spiritual practice is to strengthen our presence right here and now, being better able to handle anything that comes our way all day long.

For that reason, many of these practices are things that can be done during the course of the day, not only at some special time when you remove yourself from daily activities. For example, the best (and most difficult) time to work on anger is when you are getting angry, and so I've included a practice you can do in that very moment.

It is a mistake, however, to assume that practices will bring us to enlightenment. Genuine enlightenment — transcendence, liberation, realization, whatever one calls it — is beyond our understanding. There is no recipe, like "one cup of yoga, two tablespoons of meditation, three-quarts of prayer, a pint of service work... ."

Many people think it works like that, but it's untrue. There are karmic and cosmic forces so far beyond our understanding concerning one's "ripeness" for enlightenment, it's absurd for us to bother discussing it.

Yet clearly, spiritual practice is not entirely unrelated to one's enlightenment; if it were, then why bother doing it? Many years ago I accompanied the great rabbi Shlomo Carlebach as his guitarist. One evening in a lecture, I heard him tell the crowd, "Experiences of God can never be planned or achieved. They are spontaneous moments of grace. They are accidents."

Later that night when we were alone, I asked him, "Rabbi, why do we work so hard doing all these spiritual practices if religious experiences are just accidents?" His reply: **"To be as accident-prone as possible!"**

In other words, if we want to get hit by God's truck, go out and play on God's highway. Spiritual practices tend to keep us on the right highway; they keep us involved with the right dimension of life so that we are not constantly complicating and worsening our situation through a life of desire, fear, laziness, anger, etc.

And that's what this section of the book is about. These are simple, accessible practices which can help you do The Work all through the day. Don't overlook their depth just because they are simple. Remember that Jesus said, "Father, I thank you for concealing these truths from the clever and learned, and revealing them to the simple."

We must always feel like beginners on the Spiritual Journey. We don't need complex or esoteric practices; we certainly don't need an enormous changing variety of them. We just need to make some basic practices the very hub around which the wheel of our daily life turns. Choose some that you are drawn to, do them every day, and you *will* see changes in your own life and in the lives of people around you.

This is as practical and down-to-earth as feeding the homeless or saving the environment. And you already have everything you need in order to do it.

1. Clarifying Your Motivation

As basic as it may sound, very few people take even a few seconds every morning to remind themselves of who they are and what they hope to do with their lives, or even with that day. The mind moves toward what it dwells on. If you constantly think of illness, you're bound to get sick. And if you begin each day thinking briefly of who you are and what you most sincerely hope to find in your life, you will move toward those goals.

The Practice

1. **The Big Clarification.** Either while you're still lying in bed, or at the beginning of your morning meditation session, train yourself to bring thoughts such as these into your awareness (pause briefly between each sentence to let the meaning sink in):

    I am a seeker of truth on a spiritual journey.

    I have deep things to learn; May I learn them honorably. I have good things to offer; May I offer them generously.

    I am where I need to be; I am doing what I need to be doing.

May I be a simple, humble, kind presence on the Earth today.

May my actions today reflect my deepest beliefs.

May I be grateful to those who came before me, and may I make the roads smoother for those who will travel them after me.

2. **Little Clarifications**. Clarifying your motivation is very useful even for the small issues of daily life. As you reach for something to eat, ask yourself, what's my motivation? Am I hungry or just bored? As you go to turn on the TV, ask am I hoping to see something of value or just be distracted? In conversation, ask yourself, "What's the purpose of saying what I'm saying? Is it to share, to inspire, to help, to give, to learn — or just to compete for attention, impress others, put my two cents in?"

3. **Reviewing and Re-Dedicating Yourself for Tomorrow**. Clarifying your motivation is the front door, looking back at the end of the day is the back door. Either at the end of your evening meditation period, or when you're lying in bed before drifting off to sleep, take a few minutes to look back really honestly at the day you've just lived. His Holiness the Dalai Lama describes step three this way:

"In the late evening, look back on the day to see if you really spent your day as you pledged in the morning. If you find something positive (beneficial, helpful), then good — feel happy! Reinforce that determination by rejoicing in your own good actions and by resolving to continue such activities in the future.

"If you find you have done something negative (harmful, destructive) during the day, you should feel remorse for those wrong actions committed... reflecting on how these same negative actions, committed in the past, are the reason why you are still experiencing undesirable consequences. Think that if you continue to indulge in such activities in the future, this will lead you into similar undesirable consequences again."

This step is important, because now with compassion for yourself, you can re-dedicate your commitment for tomorrow so that you don't have to feel bad tomorrow night as well. Be honest, but gentle. Firm, but forgiving. "I'm humbled by today; may I be more consistent tomorrow for my own happiness and the happiness of all beings."

We're all weighed down by habit patterns that are hard to break. But hard or not, I promise you they are worth breaking. It's the only way we become truly new people, the only way our loftiest concepts gradually become real down to our very bones.

Remember that no one laid these hopes on you from the outside; these are the things *you* hold to be important, so as you find yourself forgetting throughout the day, it's not like "Hey stupid, look how you're not living up to whom you want to be." It's more like "Hey, remember your clarification this morning? You're not going to be happy with yourself if you violate it like this, so why not start being kind to yourself?"

Instead of being your own harshest critic, you become a gentle pal, merely reminding yourself of what you really believe in, and urging yourself to move toward it even if it's a little tough at times — well, actually, even if it's *very* tough at times.

As simple as it sounds, this is a solid beginning for living a happier, holier life. **You can't imagine how much you can really change!** You can become a happy, peaceful person no matter what you've been through, done, or feel like right now. And it may all begin very simply by clarifying your reasons for doing what you do, from big to little, every day.

2. Mountain & Wind Meditation

There are two questions about meditation that I hear quite often. One is, "how do I get my mind quiet?" The other is, "what do I do about all the noise around me?"

We're all looking for a little peace, a break from the noise around us, and from the thoughts and agitation that seem to control our minds. The problem is that, while a quiet mind may sometimes be *the result* of spiritual practice, it's very hard to "make the mind quiet." Our heart's nature is to process blood, our lungs process air, and our mind's nature is to process thoughts. We can't always do something about that. And too much of a focus on "trying to push thoughts away" will distract us from developing our meditation practice.

With that in mind, here is a practice that may help you put the noise in your mind — as well as any external noise — in perspective.

142

The Practice

1. Place your body in a comfortable meditation posture — head, neck and shoulders in a straight line, hands either folded or placed on the thighs without pulling down the shoulders. Make sure you are in a position which you won't have to move for at least fifteen minutes. If you have troubles with your knees or back, you can sit in a chair, but you still need to sit straight, so try not to use the back of the chair.

2. Pay full attention to how solid and still you feel. **Feel the body as if it were an immovable mountain.** In real fact, the body *is* like a mountain to the billions of organisms on it and inside of it. Feel this immenseness. Feel the countless life forms and activities you are hosting with no effort on your part, just like a mountain shelters herds of various animals, waterfalls, rivers, etc., yet does nothing at all. Strengthen this sense of hugeness and stability for a few minutes.

3. Begin to feel the movement of the breath, **like the steady breeze blowing across the mountain.** It is the mountain's nature not to move, while it is the wind's nature never to stop moving. Same thing with body and breath, both following their nature, both doing nothing, yet nothing remains undone.

4. If outside noise begins to intrude on your practice, or when the mind kicks in with busy thoughts, old songs, analyzing, etc., merely experience it as a radio which someone left playing in a meadow somewhere on the mountainside. It blares whatever it may be blaring, but

it has no effect on the stability of the mountain or the ceaseless flowing of the wind. The mountain doesn't think of the radio as part of itself. It doesn't try to ignore the radio, it just lets it play, remaining undisturbed by the noise. **Body sitting, breath flowing, mind playing in the background — all perfect, all peaceful, all following their nature.** Stay this way for ten to twenty minutes.

5. Toward the end of your sitting, let the breath flow a little more deeply, but slowly, and recognize how good it feels to experience your "mountain-ness" and "wind-ness." Nothing to do or stop doing, feeling very strong and solid. Notice it. Enjoy it. Let the mountain smile almost imperceptibly. Make a mental note to remember this state the next time you may be feeling small or powerless.

You are a mountain in the wind. You can handle whatever storms may pass over you, however many hikers who trample upon your surface. You are a mountain in the wind.

3. Tonglen
"Giving and Receiving"

Tonglen is an ancient Tibetan Buddhist practice which can be very powerful as a way of maintaining and strengthening a constant attitude of kindness. Our friend Evan Rotman is a serious practitioner of Buddhism. While he was in federal prison, I asked him to write this brief explanation from his own experience of adapting Tonglen to prison life. I hope it encourages you to try it.

Literally, "Tonglen" means "giving and receiving" in Tibetan. "Tong" means to give; "Len" means to receive. Although I have read many instructions for doing this form of meditation, as an incarcerated practitioner I have developed my own method that works very well for me.

It is important to have a clear state of mind before starting Tonglen, and ending the practice with the same clarity of mind. When practicing for thirty minutes, I like to just sit for ten minutes, do ten minutes of Tonglen, and bring the mind back home for ten minutes. I also break the Tonglen practice into four separate parts.

The Practice

1. ***Before you can benefit others***, *you must first have your own peace of mind. I start out by inhaling all of my own pain and confusion, filtering this "muddy" energy with love and compassion, and exhaling the pure white light energy that is inherently stashed away deep in our hearts.*

2. ***As we all know***, *there is an enormous amount of suffering in prison. I like to focus on one noisy voice in the hallway or on the tier that is obviously driven by ego-ridden pain and confusion (I've yet to have trouble picking out such a voice). Or I may think of some trivial altercation that recently occurred in the chow line, the TV room, etc. As I inhale, I concentrate on taking in all of the pain and confusion that feeds such altercations and noisy folks, and replace that pain on the exhale with warmth and compassion. With each breath, I move my concentration throughout the prison, even sharing some of this warmth with the guards, who sometimes appear to be the most confused of all.*

3. ***I then move my focus*** *beyond the prison walls to my family and friends, and to others that I may have hurt along the way. I usually end up thinking about my young son, laying in his bed at night, wondering when I'm coming home. Once again, on the inhale, I focus my attention on the muddy, smoky suffering, and I try to exhale pure white light bliss energy.*

4. **Finally, it's time to shoot the moon.** *I give a moment's thought to all of the confusion and pain in the world — from the guy in the next cell to the starving children of Rwanda, and everything in between. Once I have a clear picture of this darkness, I again inhale the pain and confusion, filter it with pure unconditional love, and exhale compassion and warmth.*

   As stated earlier, *I spend the last few minutes of my meditation practice just focusing on my breath, and bringing a sense of clarity back home.*

The really neat thing about this practice is that it's a complete tear-down of the ego. Rather than "looking out for number one," we are looking out for everyone else, by using our own heart as a filter.

The one warning I would give with the practice is not to get caught up in feeding the ego. It would be easy to give yourself praise for taking on such a practice at your own "expense." I think it's important not to conceptualize the possibility of any merit gained, but to just treat it for what it is; a practice of compassion — in the truest sense of the word, a practice.

— Evan Rotman

*Evan was released from prison in 1995 and graduated from a prestigious culinary academy in 1997. He's now the Head Chef in a Jewish retirement home.

4. Mantra

The Sanskrit word *mantra* is a combination of words which mean "mind," "sound," and "protector." Mantra can be practiced on a couple of different levels: A person may take one of the names of God as a mantra, and try to repeat it silently throughout the day. This type of mantra practice can steady the mind.

Over a long period of time, mantra can strengthen one's focus to an extraordinary degree. Mahatma Gandhi did the Classic Mantra *Ram* (God) for many years. When an assassin fatally shot him point-blank, the only thing he uttered as he crumpled to the ground was *Jai Ram* (hail God). No fear, anger, regret, just "Hail God." Imagine such unshakable presence of mind.

We can also use mantras as a practical tool for reminding ourselves of changes we're trying to make in our lives. They can help us to break through old habit patterns and old, limited ways of seeing things. The practice is separated into two parts.

148

The Practice

1. **Sit quietly** with *one* of the following mantras in the morning and repeat it to yourself for at least five minutes (longer if you can), letting the shades of meaning sink in deeper and deeper until you feel connected to what the mantra is saying to you personally. This is called "investing a mantra."

2. **After having invested the mantra**, bring it to mind as often as you can throughout the day, especially as you get caught up in the conflicts or dramas of what's going on around you. Let the mantra remind you of your deeper view, your calmer core, of the depth you may have felt during the investment period. Let it help to change your view right in the middle of all the action. It will if you stick with it.

1. ***It's Good To Be Alive.*** To be alive, to be breathing, is good. Before anything is added that causes pleasure *or* pain, harmony or conflicts, comfort or fear, success or failure; before we are old or young, black or white, rich or poor, man or woman, imprisoned or free, *It's Good To Be Alive.* In and of itself. For itself. Don't overlook it. Be grateful. If you let that most basic appreciation slide from your awareness, you will be endlessly batted back and forth like a ping-pong ball between happiness and sadness, loss and gain, pleasure and pain, constant change. The most effective way to deal with the world is to be firmly centered in life's free, basic, unchanging goodness.

In the investment period, repeat *It's Good To Be Alive*, and gradually deepen your direct, gentle experience of being alive. Feel grateful. Bring a soft smile of wisdom into your heart to start the day, knowing that today will bring ups and downs like every other day, but you will try to not be a ping-pong ball.

2. ***No Hard Feelings.*** This mantra has been powerful for a lot of people. During the investment period, as you repeat it to yourself, see how many different types of "hard feelings" come to mind. Let them all go. Even let your enemies off the hook. Soften and de-personalize such emotional states which have caused you nothing but pain for so many years.

No hard feelings. The more you see the truth of things, the easier is it to do whatever you need to do, but without self-righteousness, anger, bitterness. Every time you *feel* a harsh feeling, a hard edge, bring the mantra to mind. *No Hard Feelings.* It's tough sometimes, but it works.

3. ***Untouched.*** During the investment period, while silently repeating *untouched*, try to feel that part of you which has always been the same, through every experience of your life — that inner, unchanging witness of every moment. That is the One true, immortal Self. Take a few moments to realize that this Pure Awareness has been exactly the same during the best and worst events of your life.

Untouched. Especially when you feel extremely caught, negative or frightened, the mantra *untouched* can help you remember that it is only the character you are playing who is caught or frightened, not the Actor. The Actor, Pure Awareness, remains *untouched*. **This is a very good mantra for people who wish to be less touchy and temperamental.** Your Real Self is beyond attack.

4. **Classic Mantras.** The most traditional form of mantra is to repeat one of the names of God, or a sacred phrase containing holy words. Many people feel that the sounds of such words alone, especially in any of the ancient languages such as Arabic, Hebrew and Sanskrit, cause vibrations which affect our bodies by themselves.

You can see if one of the following mantras calls to you, or just try one anyway for a month or so, and see how it feels. These classic mantras, as well as many others, can be repeated dozens or even hundreds of times daily — waiting for a plane, in the chow line, in times of fear or stress, etc.

- *Jai Ram or Hare Krishna* (both mean "hail God" in Hindi)

- *Lord Jesus Christ, Son of God, have mercy upon me, a sinner* (this is called the "Jesus Prayer.")

- *Baruch Ata Adonai* ("Blessed are You, oh Supreme One," in Hebrew.)

- *In the Name of Allah, Most Gracious, Most Merciful* (A traditional Islamic Mantra.)

- *Om Mani Padme Hum* (Tibet's mantra of compassion.)

Mantra practice may take some time to get used to. That's why it's called practice. You may look back on your day and realize that you forgot to use your mantra at all. Feel free to use any "tricks" you can think of to do better tomorrow. A rubberband around the wrist, a watch that beeps on the hour, whatever. Your ability to remember your mantra during the craziness of the day will strengthen if you put in the effort.

5. The Richness of Poverty

Neem Karoli Baba once said to a disciple, "Serve the poor always," and the disciple said, "But Baba, who's poor?" and the great saint said, "*Everyone* is poor before Christ."

Something about that statement, "Everyone is poor before Christ" touched me deeply. I remember one day, during meditation, when I was offering everything I could think of to God — mind, body, career, family, talents, energies, time, money, thoughts, opinions, past, future, **everything** I could think of. And as I offered each thing, I saw clearly that it wasn't mine to offer in the first place. Everything I named was *already* God's, not mine!

The truth is, I had nothing to offer the One who has given me everything. I've never felt so totally poor. I saw crystal-clearly that I own nothing. The very *idea* of owning anything is ridiculous. I felt poor, and I felt ashamed having nothing to offer. And then I felt the most wonderful **poverty**. I felt the poverty of our situation, the poverty of being such utter panhandlers, receiving gifts of Grace constantly, even our every breath. I felt totally poor in Spirit, and I instantly experienced the Kingdom of Heaven. It's really true, "Blessed are the poor in spirit: for theirs is the Kingdom of Heaven"

(Matthew 5:3). Notice that Jesus didn't say, "theirs *will be* the Kingdom of Heaven;" it's not something we have to wait until we die for! The moment we really *get* our ultimate poverty before God, ours *is* the Kingdom of Heaven. For real.

The Practice

> **After a few minutes** of meditation to quiet down, begin bringing to mind anything and everything you want to offer to God or to Life, whatever word you wish to use — and then ask yourself "Does this belong to me? Did I create it? Where did I get it? Am I able to hold it or keep it from changing?" Anything you can possibly think of under the heading of "MINE," bring to mind for this practice. Where did it come from? Is it yours to keep?
>
> **With each thing that comes up**, release the idea of it being yours, release the idea of it being permanent, release the idea of having total control over its destiny. Like taking stones out of a backpack, empty out every notion of "mine" that you can locate, and move toward your empty pack, your poverty of Spirit. When you get it, you'll know it. It feels much lighter!

Then you can come back into your life as a caretaker instead of proprietor, and you'll be amazed at how much simpler and freer it feels just to work here, and not to own the shop!

6. Mother Teresa's Prayer

*W*orks of Love are Works of Peace, a recent book about the late Mother Teresa of Calcutta and her Missionaries of Charity, describes some of the prayers they use in their spiritual practice. One, called the Litany of Humility, especially caught my eye. It *seems* to be specifically geared to letting go of our whole sense of the personal self.

I urge you to spend time with this prayer, not just to read it once or twice. Reflect on each line and apply it to yourself; **notice any confusion or resentment that it brings up in you**. Give yourself time with it. Perhaps work with it every morning for a month. This prayer is so profoundly opposite our contemporary self-esteem craze that it's bound to stir up some bewilderment in us. But don't dismiss it. We don't call this spiritual *work* for nothing. It's hard!

Deliver me, O Jesus,

From the desire of being loved,
From the desire of being extolled,
From the desire of being honored,
From the desire of being praised,
From the desire of being preferred,
From the desire of being consulted,
From the desire of being approved,
From the desire of being popular,

From the fear of being humiliated,
From the fear of being despised,
From the fear of suffering rebukes,
From the fear of being calumniated,
From the fear of being forgotten,
From the fear of being wronged,
From the fear of being ridiculed,
From the fear of being suspected.

That others may be loved more than I, Jesus grant me the grace to desire it.
That others may be esteemed more than I,
That, in the opinion of the world, others may increase and I may decrease,
That others may be chosen, and I set aside,
That others may be praised, and I unnoticed,
That others may be preferred to me in everything,
That others may become holier than me, provided that I may become as holy as I should.

Our modern minds may chafe at the idea of giving up the desire to be loved, or the fear of being humiliated. We say, "But isn't that just natural? Doesn't everyone want to be loved, and want not to be humiliated?" Sure, everyone who's willing to forever feel small, limited and personal.

But spiritual teachings are not the psychology of the world. They are recipes for a fundamental transformation of who we think we are. If you truly let go of every one of the desires and fears mentioned in her prayer, you would no longer be "you," you would be the Love of God itself manifesting through this particular body and personality. Mother Teresa knew what she was praying for. This prayer is a powerful tool for changing your entire state of mind.

7. Sacred Reading

Throughout the time Josh was growing up, our primary spiritual practice together as a family was Sacred Reading. The first thing Sita, Josh and I did each morning was to gather together for a fifteen- or twenty-minute reading from a holy book.

In this way, over a period of seventeen or eighteen years, we were able to draw deep inspiration from sacred teachings such as the Bible, the Hindu *Mahabharata* and *Ramayana*, Buddhist stories, Native American tales and others. It was a wonderful way to begin each day, reminding ourselves of the biggest truths before the day's busy details began.

The Practice

With a Group: In a family or community, set time aside for daily readings. Mornings usually work best, before family or community members split off for the day. Morning readings also allow you to work with the message of the readings throughout the day.

If you'll be taking turns reading, give each person at least a week at a time — if not more — so he or she has the chance to choose longer readings and break them up over several days. Stories are often more enjoyable to read aloud than straight scripture or didactic teachings, and most good spiritual stories appeal to all ages.

By Yourself: It's really the same practice, except you'll be reading to yourself, and usually not out loud (although it's sometimes effective to read aloud even when you are alone.' That's how I write my books and newsletters). Alone, you'll have the luxury of going as slowly as you like, taking time for the reading to sink in.

Even if you can't do daily readings "together" with your friends or family, you can still do this practice long-distance with loved ones in other places. After Josh left home, he continued to read from *The Ramayana* and so did we, and we discussed it in phone calls and letters.

A Few Tips:

- Because our attention span has been under assault since the invention of television, we may not be in the habit of reading very slowly or reflectively. With this practice, remember that quantity is unimportant to what you receive from it. Classic spiritual stories, especially, are meant to be studied over and over again for a whole lifetime. As we deepen through our practices, we gain more from the same teachings each time through.

- Don't assume that the reading must hit you over the head with a blatant moral or message. Our daily life has countless subtleties, and so do holy readings. Children especially do not have to be told what it all "means." Let

159

them hear whatever they can hear. Have faith that all genuine spiritual readings have many levels of meaning.

- While there are always good contemporary spiritual books, it is also important to tap into *ancient* wisdom, such as the books and stories mentioned above, or stories from the Desert Fathers, Jataka tales, Tibetan stories, etc. It is important to see how life's most pressing concerns and personal challenges do not change over thousands of years. It helps us not get too caught up in our own era.

- Most ancient holy books are written in language which by today's standards may sound fundamentalist, sexist, or racist. While I often wince as I come across such passages, I know in my heart that the great ancient teachings have tremendous value to us underneath that old language.

We gain a lot by learning to grin and bear those turns of phrase and look deeper for the real gold hidden beneath the mud. Sacred stories have tremendous power even if they were imperfectly set down in words. It is part of our spiritual work to wrestle with passages which bother us rather than toss the teachings aside as outdated or politically incorrect, concluding that they have nothing to offer us. Such soul-searching can be a significant aspect — rather than an interruption — of the practice of Sacred Reading.

8. Two Bright Guardians

Several years ago I came across what the Buddha called "the two bright guardians of civilization." The Sanskrit words are **Hri** and **Onappa**, which translate roughly as, "Shame of having done wrong," and "Fear of doing wrong in the future." Once again, classic teachings which contradict modern thinking. Are the Buddha's teachings passé? Out of step with modern life?

Reading further, it becomes clear that the Buddha was not out of step at all. If you think about it, a truly bad person wouldn't feel shame for anything, so feeling shame or remorse is a sign that we do indeed have a decent set of values which we have violated. The point of *Hri* — shame — is to rediscover those values, to reconnect with our goodness and decency, and allow ourselves to feel the full impact of how we blew it, so we can recommit ourselves to a better life.

Likewise, a person with no wisdom, no understanding of *karma*, or "what comes around goes around," would feel no fear of doing wrong. He/she may feel fear of getting *caught*, but that's not what *Onappa* — fear of wrongdoing — is about; it's more like the old Christian term, "Godfearing."

It stands to reason that fear of the moral/spiritual consequences of doing wrong is proof that we do indeed understand the way life works: If we do wrong, we're going to suffer from it; if we do right, a better life comes of it. In that sense, fear of wrongdoing is not at all superstitious, it's an expression of faith and wisdom.

The Practice

Sit straight, quietly, as if in meditation, breathe softly and evenly with the attention focused on your heart-center. Allow yourself to reflect on the two Bright Guardians, *Hri* (shame for past actions which have been selfish, unkind, cruel, greedy, or harmful) and *Onappa* (a humble sense of caution and dread if you were to get back into that kind of behavior again).

Allow yourself to feel the fullest sense of guilt or shame you've ever felt, the fullest sense of fear over wasting your whole life in empty or immoral pursuits. Keep breathing steadily and gently into your heart, even as the old movies of your crimes or ill deeds may play on the screen of your mind. Don't jump into the screen; stay seated in your heart as you watch and accept responsibility for the choices you've made.

This is the time for no excuses, no minimizing, no self-justification at all. Feel how much you hurt. And breathing in and out of your heart, occasionally remind yourself, "I feel this bad because I really am a good person, a decent person who knows right from wrong. If I weren't a good person, I wouldn't feel so bad at having done wrong."

At some point, speak to your heart, speak to your conscience, apologize for ignoring it so many times, and ask it not to give up on you. That's when you begin working with *Onappa*, the fear of doing wrong in the future. Take a few moments to feel how scary it would be if your conscience gave up on you, think of what sort of hell you would turn your life into. That's Onappa.

Finish by praying to your own heart for help and support, and re-commit yourself to listening to your conscience, and trying not to bring more pain into the world.

If you've committed violent crimes, or other deeply regrettable acts, this process may take many sittings over a period of months or even years. But it is important and necessary work for you to do — for all of us to do, if we really want to be spiritual seekers. Wisdom and humility go hand in hand, and neither of them are possible if we're hiding from our own heart's memories and injuries.

Opening up to our shame and fear doesn't have to destroy us — that idea itself is just fear. **On the contrary, opening up allows us to recognize and accept the sum total of who we are.** We are holy. But we have all done enough harm that none of us should ever be smug. That's how these two ancient "bright guardians of civilization" can help us regain humility for ourselves and for our troubled society.

9. Practicing The Presence Of God

What would you do, how do you think you'd behave, if you could *see* God or *feel* God with you right now — literally, physically, right here? The Sacred One. The Holy. Right here, right now.

At the very least, you'd probably feel hushed, humbled and grateful. Every complaint would vanish from your mind. Your actions would probably be unselfish. If somebody offended you, you'd likely forgive them. Out of respect, you'd take good care of yourself. If you had to stand up against corruption or evil, you'd courageously do the right thing, because you would see that God knows, and God guides you, even when things *seem* horrible, scary or sad. God's sacred presence would bring you peace and comfort, even if you were dying of AIDS, or losing your job, or being executed by the state.

Well, the scriptures of *every* religion tell us it's literally true — **God is here with us at every moment**. They also assure us that by Grace, each one of us can actually experience God directly; we can *know* God first-hand — what I call *touching the Sacred.*

This experience was the way of life in most Native American faiths. Walking Buffalo, a Stoney Indian said, "We see the Great Spirit's work in everything: sun, moon, trees, wind, and mountains. Sometimes we approached him through these things. From this we have a true belief in the Supreme Being."

The actual experience may be a ways off for most of us, but we can *practice* this presence of God to develop an awareness and lifestyle more in keeping with how holy everything really is. Try it yourself and see the difference it makes in your life.

The Practice

Remind yourself dozens or even hundreds of times throughout the day, *God is here, right now. The Holy Father, the Divine Mother, the Messiah, is with me. Everything I think, do or say is in the presence of a loving God. Nothing is unimportant. No one is meaningless. Everything counts. I want to act accordingly.*

Recognize that the same is true for everyone else, whether they know it or not. Even when you're struggling with another person, remember that *God is here, watching and loving us both.* So respect the conflict without wasting energy rejecting it, like "this shouldn't be happening." God knows what is important for us to experience. God knows.

That's it. Simple, huh? The presence of God can be practiced anywhere, anytime, because nothing is excluded. Look around you right now. You're on hallowed ground. God is here. Our spiritual journey is not to make anything more holy, but only to drop every barrier, every addiction, every bit of pettiness, gossip, greed, pride, and delusion, which blocks us from seeing how holy everything already *is*. Practicing the presence of God is a very appropriate thing to do.

10. Working With Anger

It's very difficult to exercise self-discipline in the middle of anger, but you can do it. You must move your attention from the **object** of your anger, to the **process** of it instead. Forget who did what to whom. You can deal with that later, when you're calmer and less likely to make things worse. For now, focus on the experience as an observer, not as hero or victim. Study this fascinating thing called anger.

The Practice

As you feel yourself getting angry, stay still, try to breathe more smoothly and just a little more deeply.

Then allow yourself to feel the tightness in your stomach, neck and shoulders, the bitterness, the adrenaline, the indignant "rightness," the unfairness and injustice huffing and puffing around in your head.

Next, become aware of the terrible separateness which anger creates, not just between you and the object of your anger, but between you and your own body, between you and the whole universe. Observe what anger really feels like in all its aspects.

Now, as you allow all these awful feelings to come into awareness, remind yourself, "Anger feels terrible! All people feel like this at one time or another. May I be more compassionate. May I use this anger to help me feel what I have in common with all beings."

Finally, if you know someone who is especially angry much of the time, take a moment to focus on him specifically with a prayer of Goodwill, like "May this experience help me to be more compassionate to so-and-so. May it remove some of his anger." Hold the image of that person as clearly as you can, and try to remove his anger by seeing his tightness relax and his face soften. Then shower and surround him with understanding and peace.

End with a prayer of Goodwill, something like, "May the anger I have felt, serve to relieve someone else of having to feel it. May this experience help to lessen the amount of anger in the world, and lessen the power of anger over all people."

In order to understand the suffering which anger produces in countless human beings, we must set aside our personal response to it long enough to feel and understand the whole phenomenon more clearly. When we do this, anger no longer controls us as it once did, because we see all the falsehoods involved and all the ways we have tricked ourselves into acting blindly or hysterically. This practice can be a giant step toward true freedom.

11. Breaking Free

It can be a bit overwhelming to talk conceptually about simplifying our lives. However, once we take it out of the abstract, we see the process entails nothing more than some straightforward and *simple* steps toward living more in tune with our beliefs. Here are a few ways to begin.

The Practice

1. **Get Out of Debt and Stay Out!** Pay off your debts and then live within your means. If you can't afford it, don't buy it. Other than a home or land, never buy anything on time, even a car. You will discover many good things about yourself if you follow this advice. Your kids will benefit greatly. Especially never go into debt for a wedding or graduation, for tuxes, gowns, limos, etc. It creates stress and reinforces distorted views about "the good life." Celebrate special affairs with potlucks, picnics, and other happy, stress-free events.

2. **Buy One, Give Away One.** Get into the habit of giving away one old item for each new item you buy. Want a new CD? Give away — or sell — an old one. New shirt? Shoes? Same thing. Your kids will learn a

lot from this, and your home will be less cluttered. When you're ready to reduce clutter even more, give *two* away for every one you buy. It is a wonderful feeling not to be burdened by too many possessions. This practice also helps you think twice before buying!

3. **Team Up With Friends and Neighbors.** Carpooling, trading goods and services, even buying a home or a piece of land to live on with friends — there are many ways you can save money by joining with others. Begin by having open discussions about what you all spend money on. Many ways to save will become obvious. We must overcome our contemporary attitude of not wanting to share and not wanting to depend on each other. It hasn't worked. We need to need each other.

4. **Quit Smoking and Drinking!** Over 60 million Americans, including most prison inmates, smoke. A pack-a-day smoker these days is spending about $60 per month, or $720 per year. Double that amount for two people in the same family, or if you smoke a couple packs a day. Add in a similar amount for beer, wine, or liquor, and you can see that many people who may consider themselves poor are working about a quarter of their time to pay for these habits which shorten their lives, weaken their health, and provide a bad example for their children. Voluntary, suicidal slavery.

Many prisoners say they wish they could do more for their kids, yet they take serious amounts of money from their families for cigarettes. Talk is cheap. There's no better way to show you've really changed than to give up smoking and devote that money to your kids, or to a cause you believe in. This is not just about alcohol or tobacco; it's about taking control of our lives.

5. **Boycott Holiday Buying Madness Forever.** Think about how much of your annual salary you spend on things that break and rust. Sita, Josh and I agreed years ago not to buy gifts for each other on birthdays or holidays. What a relief! And believe it or not, your friends and family will survive the shock if you extend it to them as well. We make plans to be with each other and **do** something together instead of rushing to the mall to buy meaningless junk. We make something ourselves, or prepare a favorite meal.

There's no way around the fact that we can't have everything. Much of the joy of simpler living is to *love* the old car that's paid for; to *enjoy* the old sofa from the thrift shop; to *appreciate* the simple home-cooked meals.

Whether it's cars or clothes or furniture, we need to strengthen our *inner* dignity so that we are no longer slaves to fashion. We must rethink our basic values and help our kids form a deeper sense of self-worth than the cost of the clothes they wear. Be bold. It's time to take a stand toward simpler living even if it's hard to do. It's the only way to break free from the mass hypnosis of modern advertising and obsessive consumerism.

12. Vow Practice

Many of us complain about how hard it is to quit smoking or lying or masturbating, or to start meditating, jogging, eating right — any number of things connected to "turning over a new leaf." We may make solemn resolutions, but within a short time we often find everything is back to the way it was. Then we gradually become cynical and conclude that we may as well give up; that "we'll never change."

Vow practice is more formal than making verbal resolutions. Most of us at Human Kindness Foundation work with vow practice and we have found it extremely helpful for making real and lasting changes. The basic elements of the practice are **Preparation**, **Declaration**, and **Implementation**:

The Practice

Preparation: Plan ahead a week or two. Vows taken impulsively (or angrily!) usually don't last. Spend time in prayer and reflection about any changes you want to make — major or minor, lifelong or temporary. Think ahead to the ways this vow may affect your life, your friendships, future plans, etc., and accept those consequences. There is no gain without some amount of sacrifice or loss.

Then work on the wording of your vow. One inmate friend wanted to take a vow of total silence for a year. I said, "What if a C.O. speaks to you and requires you to answer?" We advised him to do two things: Include in the wording of his vow something like "except in cases of genuine emergency or having to respond to an official;" and we also suggested he let the warden know about his desire to take a vow of silence, and ask for his cooperation. Mature planning makes for a mature vow.

The most important thing about a vow is, don't take it until you know you will keep it. So if you're unsure of whether you can live up to "I will always..." or "I will never..." then use the wording **"I will strive to..."** That way, your sworn commitment is to *try*, and sometimes this may actually work better anyway.

Make a practical time limit also. If the idea of quitting smoking "forever" is too scary, make a vow not to smoke for one month, or one week – even a day if that's all you think you can do.

Honoring our promises is essential for self-respect and any success in life. So, think carefully about your vows, and discuss them with someone you trust. That's the step of preparation.

Declaration: Once a vow has been properly prepared, the next step is to "declare it" in a little ceremony with one or more friends as witnesses. This is important, because like a marriage ceremony, you are obligating yourself publicly to follow your vow. If you break it, others will know you have let yourself down. You will have let them down as well, because they may not have as much faith in themselves after seeing you break your vow.

It is important to commit ourselves in front of others, and it is also very encouraging to know they support our struggle to abide by the promises we have made. After you declare your vow, the witness or other friends can just say something like, "We respect your vow, and we receive your vow." In my own community, that's the step of declaration. We usually do this while bowing to each other with respect.

Implementation: Then comes the bottom line: Day by day, abiding by the vow you have taken. **I strongly encourage you to repeat your vow out loud, alone, at the beginning of every day.** Read it or recite it as sincerely as you did that first day, and remember the feelings which prompted you to take this vow. If you are in a dormitory situation, you may have to do this in a whisper, sitting up in bed, facing a wall, or whatever — but it's very useful to repeat your vow every day. That way, you are actually *taking* the vow every day.

This would be a powerful practice even for marriage vows: Both husband and wife repeating their vows to each other every morning of their lives. Believe it or not, although it sounds like it would get stale, daily repetition is actually a way to keep the vows very fresh (and that's a good reason for vows to be worded briefly instead of long, dramatic declarations).

Sita and I do this practice even after thirty-two years of marriage. At the beginning of each day, we face each other and clasp hands, look into each other's eyes, and say, **"May I truly cherish you today, knowing this may be our last day together."** It's a very useful and powerful practice.

Remember to respect all vows equally. Whether you vow to stop eating sweets for a week, or to never take a sip of alcohol for the rest of your life, a vow must be respected fully. A sincere vow is an expression of our willingness to work, to sacrifice, to change. It shows that we understand how life works — that change doesn't come just because we whine about it. Real, lasting change requires planning, effort, and perseverance.

A vow is also a great way to initiate yourself into daily spiritual practice. Vow to do any of the practices in this book, at the same time each day for three months. Then, whether you are sick or well, tired or alert, bored or restless, you just do it. It doesn't matter whether you feel like it, or whether it seems to be doing you any good, or whether you're good at it; you've taken a vow to do it anyway. What a relief! Vow practice gives us a major freedom to change our lives by giving up some minor freedoms of changing our minds. Try it and see.

Conclusion:
What Has Been Said?

With all this talking,
What has been said?

— Lao Tzu, *Hua Hu Ching*

And so we come to the end of one more book. I am always a little reluctant to produce another book (that's why this is only my fourth in twenty-five years), because I ask myself certain questions which are tough to answer:

Has anything been said which has not already been said countless times before? No. Has anything been said which will help the reader in and of itself? Words can certainly help us, but not for very long.

Was the publication of this book worth the trees which were cut down for the paper it is written on? That is a tough question, because it doesn't only depend on whether I have written anything decent. It also depends on whether you, the reader, decide to use the ideas and practices in this book to help create a deeper, simpler, more peaceful world. My karma as a tree-killer is in your hands.

It is, of course, my fondest hope that you allow these teachings I've passed along from the Great Traditions to inspire you to take action both on the inner plane of your spiritual life and in the outer world as well.

Believe me, I know how much easier it is to read about it (and to write about it!) than to do it. I know how unbelievably hard it can be to change our lives in major ways. I know how easy it is to be cynical about trying yet one more round of ideas or practices or vows or new year's resolutions; we've jerked ourselves around for so many years; we've failed so many times.

You and I both know these things because we are human beings, and this is how things are for human beings. A spiritual life is pretty demanding and takes a lot of personal struggle no matter how many fine books you may read or workshops you may attend.

Give Me One Good Reason...

Many unhappy people have asked me to give them one good reason to believe in anything deep, or to try any of this difficult spiritual work. I can actually give two good reasons:

First, **Holiness exists**, and it is worth any amount of effort or sacrifice to experience it. I have personally experienced states of profound closeness to God, satori, rigpa, bliss, ecstasy, rapture — whatever favorite words you may have for mystical experiences which take you out of the individual self and plunk you down in the middle of the Goodness of the Universe. So I know that all this stuff is real. It's not just poetry or wishful thinking.

Secondly, Sita and I have been fortunate to meet spiritual elders of many traditions; people who embody the very best of what it means to be a human being. They all assure us that **you and I are also on our way toward becoming holy elders** just like them. It is not only possible, it is our duty. Look around: Is there any other type of success which is worth striving for? Any other path which looks misery or death square in the face and smiles serenely, fearlessly?

Just A Timely Reminder

So what has been said? Nothing new, nothing earth-shattering; just a timely reminder of the truths we know deep in our bones but are so clever at avoiding! And now it's back into the arena of our lives, where we get a chance to reflect or reject these age-old truths all through the day.

I hope you try some of the practices in your daily life. I know first-hand that daily practice is an effective way to combat old habit patterns that keep dragging us down. On our way toward becoming free of all habitual behavior, it is often necessary to first replace bad habits with good ones. The habit of spiritual practice — especially at the very beginning of each day — can remind us of who we are and what we wish our lives to be about.

We can be deep people at the same time as remaining simple, almost childlike in our faith. A deep and simple life is a life well lived, and service to others then flows naturally out of it in all directions. In the end, simplicity, practice and service are seen to be a perfectly normal way of life, leading to great satisfaction rather than nostalgia and regret. No one can block us from this time-honored path. The choice is ours.

Human Kindness Foundation

Human Kindness Foundation is a non-profit organization dedicated to the three principles expressed in this book: personal spiritual practice; simple, modest living; and unselfish service to others.

We publish Bo Lozoff's books and other materials, offering them free to prisoners, prison staff, and anyone who genuinely can't afford to pay for them. We also have an online store which offers our materials for purchase, as well as other books, CDs, and DVDs which we consider to be valuable spiritual teachings. Go to **www.humankindness.org** and click on HKF Store.

Our free newsletter, *A Little Good News*, is published three times each year. Anyone in or out of prison is welcome to be on our mailing list for the newsletter. As of 2009, our mailing list numbers about 45,000 people from all walks of life.

Human Kindness Foundation is supported by the affectionate generosity of people who believe in our work. We do no fundraising or grantwriting. If you would like to help financially, your contribution is most welcome. All donations are fully tax-deductible as per IRS regulations for 501(c)(3) charities. Buying books, t-shirts and other items from our store is another way to support our work. For all inquiries, please contact us at:

Human Kindness Foundation,
PO Box 61619, Durham NC 27715
phone (919) 383-5160   fax (919) 383-5140
www.humankindness.org